THE GREAT ENCOUNTER OF CHINA
AND THE WEST, 1500–1800

Critical Issues in History

The British Imperial Century, 1815–1914: A World History Perspective
   by Timothy H. Parsons

The Great Encounter of China and the West, 1500–1800
   by D. E. Mungello

THE GREAT ENCOUNTER OF CHINA AND THE WEST, 1500–1800

D. E. Mungello

ROWMAN & LITTLEFIELD PUBLISHERS, INC.
Lanham • New York • Boulder • Oxford

ROWMAN & LITTLEFIELD PUBLISHERS, INC.

Published in the United States of America
by Rowman & Littlefield Publishers, Inc.
4720 Boston Way, Lanham, Maryland 20706

12 Hid's Copse Road
Cumnor Hill, Oxford OX2 9JJ, England

British Library Cataloguing in Publication Information Available

Library of Congress Cataloging-in-Publication Data

Mungello, David E., 1943–
      The great encounter of China and the West, 1500–1800 / D. E.
Mungello
          p.   cm. — (Critical issues in history)
      Includes bibliographical references and index.
      ISBN 0-8476-9439-9 (alk. paper). — ISBN 0-8476-9440-2
(paper: alk. paper)
          1. China—Civilization—Western influence.   2. Europe—Civilization—
Chinese influences.   3. East and West.   4. China—History—Ming dynasty,
1368–1644.   5. China—History—Ch'ing dynasty, 1644–1912.   I. Title.   II.
Series.
      DS750.72.M86   1999
      951—dc21   99-12405
                                                                                  CIP

Printed in the United States of America

♾ ™ The paper used in this publication meets the minimum requirements of
American National Standard for Information Sciences—Permanence of Paper for
Printed Library Materials, ANSI Z39.48–1984.

Contents

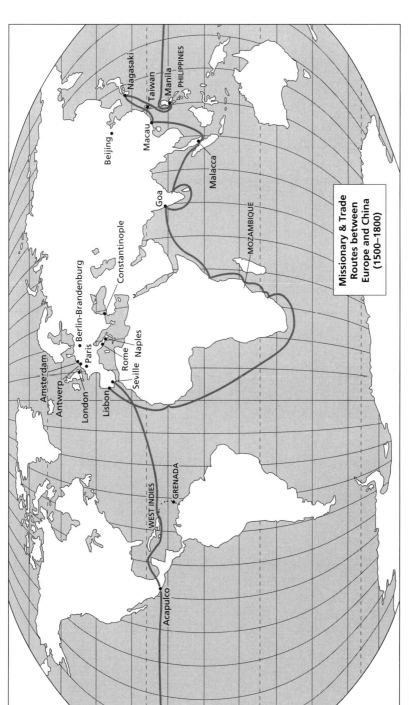

Missionary & Trade
Routes between
Europe and China
(1500–1800)

Map 1

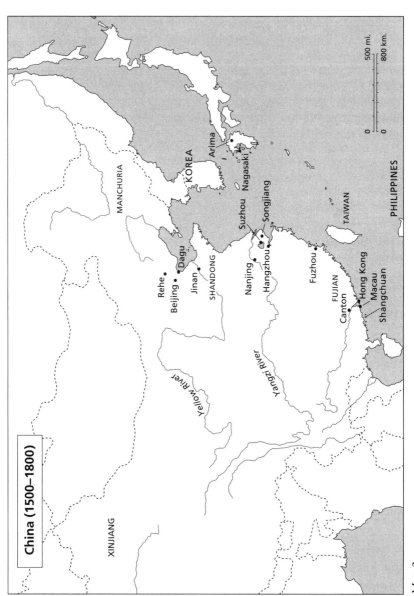

China (1500–1800)

XINJIANG

Yellow River

Yangzi River

MANCHURIA

Rehe
Beijing
Dagu
Jinan
SHANDONG

KOREA

Arima
Suzhou Nagasaki
Songjiang
Nanjing
Hangzhou

Fuzhou

TAIWAN

FUJIAN
Canton
Hong Kong
Macau
Shangchuan

PHILIPPINES

500 mi.
800 km.

Map 2

Illustrations

Series Editor's Foreword

As historian Jonathan D. Spence observes, "Westerners have been unclear about China since they first began to live there in any numbers and to write about the country at length."[1] Indeed, many in the West would dismiss the first full report of China written in the mid-fourteenth century by Marco Polo, whose tales of the vast wealth, power, and strange customs of the country under Mongol rule appeared so fantastic as to be fiction. Following the collapse of the Mongol empire and the disruption of known trade routes, China faded in European memory until the mid-sixteenth century when European traders and missionaries once again began to travel to the East in search of wealth and with glorious aspirations of converting China to Christianity. This renewed encounter between East and West brought together two cultures assured of their own cosmological superiority and historical destiny. The impact of this meeting affected the perceptions of each toward the other by challenging, as well as reinforcing, their own cultural assumptions of superiority; nonetheless, in the process, their historical destinies would be changed inalterably.

For Westerners, China remained enigmatic. Impressed with the cultivated politeness, refined manners, and elegance of Chinese culture, many Europeans constructed China into a mirror used to reflect and accentuate the foibles and presumptions of the West. So impressed were many with the arts and sciences of China that some Western students concluded that they would rather have been born in China than in the West. Furthermore, as Spence notes, early studies of the language and culture led a number of theorists of "colossal eccentricity" to a variety of conclusions: Chinese was the "mother" language of all others, an old Hebrew dialect, a parallel language of the Goths, or a language to be deciphered by mathematics or musical scales.[2]

While in awe of the vastness and diversity of China, the early Jesuit missionaries to China noted its dark side as well. Appreciation for China's ethical system and the ideal of a scholarly mandarinate found expression in early Jesuit writings, but infanticide, the sale of children, and prostitution were grimly noted as well. Similarly, French Enlightenment thinkers contrasted an ethically moral Chinese society with the corruption of Catholic Europe, while Americans such as Benjamin Franklin and Thomas Jefferson spoke in admiration of China's aged laws and of the "natural aristocracy" of the Chinese. Nevertheless, English naval officer George Anson, visiting Canton in the 1740s, denigrated China as a land inhabited by a submissive population ruled by contemptible officials. Jean-Jacques Rousseau, Nicolas Boulanger, and G. W. F. Hegel saw in China an example of Asian despotism. A chorus of early-nineteenth-century writers, including Charles Dickens, Ralph Waldo Emerson, and Karl Marx, derided Chinese morality and the country's economic backwardness. In the late nineteenth century, racist denunciations of Chinese immigrants led to exaggerated fears of "mongolization," disease, and foreign invasion. Thus the Western response remained ambivalent at best, vacillating at times between laudatory awe of the strange and mysterious East and fear and loathing of a corrupt, stagnant civilization.

Yet the Chinese response to the West remained even less positive. The Chinese saw European visitors as "barbarians," notably for their uncivilized behavior, ugly facial features, and distinctively pungent body odors. Europeans were labeled "ghosts," a reference to their white skins, a term that held deep derogatory connotations in the Chinese spiritual world. When the first Jesuit missionaries arrived in the late 1500s, China was becoming isolationist, restricting trade and travel for all foreigners. In turn, the Chinese government discouraged its own people from traveling abroad. European industry, such as watchmaking, attracted the emperor's interest, but attempts to develop this craft in China were thwarted by a rigid and myopic bureaucracy. European sciences, such as chemistry, also failed to take hold in China. Europeans introduced to Chinese painting the concept of perspective, but European art often met with resistance and had minimal influence. Christianity met with open hostility, often polemical and sometimes violent. In the nineteenth and twentieth centuries, many Chinese came to admire Western industry and "know-how," but others denounced the West as overly materialistic, avaricious, and morally decadent.

The profound difference in Chinese and Western cultures can be seen in the symbol of the Christian crucifix itself. Westerners saw in the Cross the embodiment of sacrifice, in which the Son of God experienced humiliation and death to free humanity from its natural state of sin. Westerners saw in Christ's death salvation and grace. For the Chinese, with their profound sense of social order and fear of banditry, the Cross represented rebellion and subversion. What kind of religion is it, Chinese scholars asked, that worships a criminal who proclaims himself a lord and calls upon his followers to renounce their families and their past lives? From the Chinese perspective, one of the most remarkable features of Christianity in China was not that the missionaries believed that this vast nation could be won to the Christian faith but that any conversions took place at all.

The interaction of Western and Chinese cultures remains complex and multidimensional, with each side exerting influence on the other. D. E. Mungello, in tracing these early encounters of the West with China, introduces readers to this powerful engagement between two cultures. Europeans, as Mungello explains, found China in the mid-fifteenth century flourishing in population, commerce and industry, the arts, and literature. Yet China increasingly turned inward in this period, as the Ming dynasty imposed bans on coastal and foreign trading. The conquest of China by the Manchus, who established the new Qing dynasty in 1644, brought further ruin to China's maritime trade, thereby allowing the Portuguese, Spanish, and Dutch to fill a vacuum. This commercial relationship between China and European traders opened new opportunities for cultural exchange, as well as creating occasions for political confrontations and military engagements. In the ebb and flow of Chinese-European relations, Mungello finds, cultural borrowing and assimilation were apparent in both directions. Mungello's vivid portrait of the encounter of China and the West, I believe, will encourage his readers to want to discover more about this early relationship between China and Europe and the difficulties of cultural interaction and its implications for the diverse world in which we now live.

—DONALD T. CRITCHLOW
SERIES EDITOR

Notes

1. Jonathan D. Spence, "Looking East: The Long View," in *Chinese Roundabout: Essays in History and Culture* (New York: W. W. Norton, 1992), 78–90.
2. Spence, "Introduction," in *Chinese Roundabout,* 4.

Preface

This book represents the results of twenty-nine years of research in the field of early modern Sino-Western history. When I first began studying the field as a graduate student at Berkeley in 1970, I wished to communicate only with a very small circle of specialists. However, over the years, I have felt compelled to explain these results to a broader audience. The Critical Issues in History series of Rowman & Littlefield Publishers has given me this opportunity. Whether I have succeeded in my attempt to reach a broader readership will be up to the reader to judge.

Thus, this book is written for the history student and the general reader. Because the aim is to present information and ideas in the clearest and most meaningful manner, I have reduced the scholarly apparatus to a minimum. There are no footnotes. I am not altogether comfortable with omitting a detailed listing of my scholarly debts in footnote form, but I hope this omission may be excused by the aims of the book. I would like to emphasize here that scholarship is a corporate enterprise and my debt to many other scholars is enormous. The numerous sources that I consulted are listed at the end of each chapter, and technical terms are explained in the text. Although the technicalities have been reduced to a minimum, the ideas in this book are intended to be substantive and challenging.

The most common way of referring to a Chinese emperor since the Ming dynasty (1368–1644) is by his reign-title *(nianhao)* rather than his given name. The term "Kangxi" is a reign-title rather than a name; for this reason, I refer to the "Kangxi Emperor" rather than to "Emperor Kangxi." Similarly, we would refer to President Franklin Delano Roosevelt as the "New Deal president" rather than "President New Deal." Of course, the Kangxi Emperor had a name, several in fact. He was formally named Xuanye and he is sometimes called by his posthumous temple-name Emperor Shengzu, but this is a complication that is best avoided in such a short work. The same situation applies to other emperors mentioned in this book, such as the Chongzhen Emperor, the Shunzhi Emperor, and the Qianlong Emperor. The Pinyin system of romanization of Chinese characters has been used.

The most frustrating effort in producing this book has been my failure to identify the source of the cartoon "The Miracle Teapot," which appears in figure 1.3 and on the front cover. I have corresponded with a number of China scholars and archivists, only to end up with the following information. The cartoon appeared in the English-language edition of Jean Chesneaux's *Peasant Revolts in China, 1840–1949* (London: Thames & Hudson, 1973). An American edition was published by W. W. Norton of New York in the same year. Neither the author nor the translator, C. A. Curwen, was involved in the selection of illustrations. This was done entirely by the London publisher, Thames & Hudson. The picture research was done by Célestine Dars, apparently from materials available in archives in London. "The Miracle Teapot" is identified in the list of illustrations in that book on page 172 as a "Russian cartoon, c. 1901. Church Missionary Society." The contents of the cartoon appear quite clearly to refer to the events of the Boxer Rebellion in north China in 1898 through 1901.

Unfortunately, I have not been able to locate any such organization with the name "Church Missionary Society." The cartoon is not in the London Missionary Society archives held in the School of Oriental and African Studies at the University of London. There were two Church of England missions in China in 1901. One was the Church Mission Society (Low Church) and the other was the Society for the Propagation of the Gospel in Foreign Parts (SPGFP) (High Church). The cartoon is not in the archives of the Church Mission Society at the University of Birmingham, although the London archivist at the time (1973) recalls providing Thames & Hudson with illustrations that did not include "The Miracle Teapot." The archives of the SPGFP at Oxford contain only letters and not images, and the archivist is not familiar with the cartoon, although she noted that the Society did have missionaries who were murdered at the time of the Boxer Rebellion in China. The publishing house of Thames & London has not provided clarification. So while the cartoon appears likely to date from 1901 and is possibly Russian in origin, I cannot provide further information.

I am grateful to the editor of the Critical Issues in History series, Professor Donald T. Critchlow of Saint Louis University, for inviting me to write this book. I would like to thank the Rowman & Littlefield staff for their assistance, particularly Mr. Stephen M. Wrinn, acquisitions editor, and Ms. Lynn Weber, production editor; and Ms. Cheryl W. Hoffman of Hoffman-Paulson Associates, copyeditor. I am indebted to Dr. Gail King, the Asian Collection curator of the Harold B. Lee Library, Brigham Young University, for her assistance in obtaining the illustration of Madame Candida Xu; to Mr. Eugenio Menegon for his assistance in clarifying the exact location of the Chinese portrait of Father G. Aleni; and to Dr. R. G. Tiedemann of the University of London for his assistance in searching the British archives for the source of the cartoon "The Miracle Teapot." Finally, I would like to express my gratitude to Baylor University and to the Department of History for their support of this project.

In 1977 my first book was dedicated to my wife, and now this book is dedicated to her memory. Christine McKegg Mungello (1946–1997), *requiescat in pace.*

1

Historical Overview

In 1453 the Byzantine capital, Constantinople, finally fell to the Ottoman Turks and a great historical, religious, political, and commercial bastion was detached from the rest of European civilization. Eastern and central Europe would now be threatened by the Muslim Turks for the next two centuries. In many respects, this was the nadir of European civilization in early modern history. At this point, Europe's greatness was a memory of the past and its future ascent was not yet visible. By contrast, in 1453 no nation in the world shined brighter than China. By standard criteria such as size, population, agriculture, commerce, wealth, sophistication, technology, military might, cuisine, learning, literature, and the fine arts, the Ming dynasty presided over the greatest nation in the world. (In retrospect, we know that China had entered into a long and gradual decline in many of these areas, but this decline would not become apparent until nearly 1800.)

Europe and China had engaged in trade along the Silk Route since the Roman and Han empires had pacified either end of Eurasia, but there were no substantive intellectual or cultural exchanges until after 1500. The Chinese had the ability to mount distant naval voyages and had done so in the years 1405–1433 when enormous Chinese fleets traveled throughout the Indian Ocean as far as southern Arabia, east Africa, and Mozambique. However, after these voyages ended, China's cultural and political preeminence, wealth, and concern with external threats to its security combined to cause the Chinese to turn inward. When the Portuguese explorer Vasco da Gama sailed around southern Africa and on to India in 1498, there were few signs left to indicate to Europeans that the Chinese had made voyages in this region earlier in that century.

The Ming dynasty (1368–1644) had been established by some remarkably capable rulers who had organized a system of government that would last, largely unchanged, for over five hundred years. The foundations of the Ming were so well laid that the positive effects of good government and prosperity would continue for two centuries, or well into the sixteenth century. Agriculture thrived under the attention of a government that repaired and expanded canals and irrigation works and stocked public granaries. New strains of rice imported from Southeast Asia and new crops (maize, peanuts, and potatoes) imported from the Americas by way of the Philippines increased the food supply. The result was a healthier and more numerous population. Although commerce was disparaged by Confucian morality, it flourished. The Chinese export of silk, tea, and porcelains—the envy of the world—produced such a flow of silver from Spanish mines in Mexico and Peru that it, along with copper, displaced paper money. The emergence of silver as a prime form of currency was one of the more important events in Ming monetary history.

The Chinese view of the rest of the world in 1500 was a result of approximately thirty-five hundred years of historical development in which Chinese culture was the dominant influence in East Asia. Nations like Japan, Korea, and Vietnam all had been fundamentally shaped by the written Chinese language, by the Chinese imperial system, and by Confucian teachings that emphasized, on one hand, a hierarchical family, political, and social order and, on the other hand, the selection of government officials on the egalitarian principle of literary examinations.

During China's early history, geographical separation from the rest of the world had fostered a Chinese ethnocentrism, or Sinocentrism. Chinese regarded their country as the center of the world and named it the "Middle Kingdom" (Zhongguo), in contrast to the "foreign kingdoms" (waiguo) in the rest of the world. The Chinese emperor, referred to as the "Son of Heaven" (Tianzi), was believed to rule with the mandate and authority of Heaven. According to traditional Chinese cosmology, the organization of mankind on the earth should duplicate the pattern found in the heavens. In this way of thinking, the Chinese emperor was compared to the polestar. Just as the other stars revolved around it, so too did other humans revolve in hierarchical order around the emperor. China's view of the rest of the world was an extension of this system in terms of seeing other countries in a hierarchical and nonegalitarian manner.

For China, the non-Chinese world consisted of three zones. The first included a Sinitic zone of countries that were the closest geographically and that had borrowed extensively from Chinese culture. These included Korea, Vietnam, the Liuqiu (Ryukyu) Islands, and sometimes Japan. The second was an Inner Asian zone that consisted of people who were both ethnically and culturally non-Chinese. Whereas the Sinitic zone bordered on the east and south of China, the Inner Asian zone bordered on the north and west. The third division was an outer zone that consisted of "outer barbarians" (waiyi) and included Southeast Asia, South Asia, and Europe.

The Chinese viewed all non-Chinese states as inferior and expected them, at least in theory, to be tributary states. The Chinese emperor was supposed to rule by virtue of his superior human qualities. The favor that he bestowed was to be dispensed not only to Chinese but also to barbarians. To receive this imperial favor, the barbarians were to travel to the imperial court "to be transformed" *(laihua)*. Over the centuries, these foreign lands sent embassies to the Chinese capital carrying gifts in the form of tribute signifying their subservient status to the Chinese. In turn, they received the rewards of the emperor's benevolent paternalism, which sometimes represented an amount that had been previously negotiated to appease a foreign military threat to the Chinese. The court reception of these foreign embassies involved an elaborate ritual that required foreigners to perform the kowtow *(koutou)*, a triple genuflection and touching of the head to the ground nine times. Oftentimes these embassies included merchants who were allowed to trade within clearly defined limits. Down through Chinese history, the reality of these foreign embassies did not always fit the theory, but the theory of Sinocentrism persisted into the nineteenth century. (The root "Sino" [Chinese] and terms such as "Sinology" [the study of China] are derived from the Latin term for "Chinese," *Sinae*.)

In spite of China's ethnocentrism, the Chinese did have substantive contact with Central and South Asians during the first millennium of our era. During that time, Buddhism entered China and was assimilated into Chinese culture. The Tang dynasty (618–907) was one of the most cosmopolitan periods in Chinese history, and the influence of Buddhism peaked. Not only was there contact with India, Persia, and even Byzantium via the old Silk Route through Central Asia, but also numerous Arab traders from the Red Sea area established communities in southern Chinese ports. There was also extensive contact with Japan. Tang ceramic figurines portray a variety of peoples.

Although Chinese merchants wished to trade abroad, they were restricted by the Ming government from doing so. Throughout the fourteenth century, a series of trade limitations was imposed; for example, in 1394, ordinary Chinese were prohibited from using foreign perfumes and other foreign goods. Foreign trade was restricted to those lands that stood in a tributary relationship to China. The pressure to trade became so great in the sixteenth century and the government's efforts to combat smuggling so fruitless that the ban on trading was partially lifted in 1567. The government attempted to control trade through a system of licensing private traders. All other traders who ventured abroad did so under threat of severe penalties, including beheading. Confucianism contained a strong philosophical bias against merchants, on the grounds that they were motivated by profit rather than human benevolence. Traditionally, merchants were ranked last (after literati, peasants, and craftsmen) among the four main classes. And yet the potential wealth to be obtained through commerce was so great that many people became merchants in spite of the obstacles and because of practical realities. Many literati who served as scholar-officials closed their eyes to numerous violations of the prohibitions on trade.

By the end of the Ming dynasty, the bans on coastal and foreign trade had been reimposed and the Chinese who engaged in foreign trade were practically indistinguishable from pirates. The first Chinese to settle Taiwan were a blend of pirates and merchants of contraband. In 1620–1660 a severe depression in the worldwide trading system disrupted the flow of silver into China, mainly from the Americas, and appears to have worsened inflation in the late Ming. The deterioration of the quality of Ming emperors and their inability to respond to problems hastened social disintegration. These conditions made it possible for the Manchus, a Tungusic tribal people who had been emerging to the northeast of China in present-day Manchuria, to move their armies into China. When the Manchus conquered the Ming capital of Beijing and established the Qing dynasty in 1644, the traders and pirates on the southeast coast allied themselves with the Ming loyalists. They were led in their fight against the Manchus by the swashbuckling pirate Zheng Chenggong (1624–1662), known in European accounts as Koxinga. Born to a Chinese father and a Japanese mother, Zheng was one of the first of a category of Chinese who lived abroad called "Overseas Chinese."

The exalted Manchu fighting prowess did not extend to sea warfare, and after suffering a series of humiliating naval defeats, the Manchus shifted tactics in 1660 and began evacuating the population from Chinese coastal areas ten miles inland to deprive these traders and pirates of their food and other supplies. The government burned the coastal towns and destroyed the local inhabitants' boats. This policy had the effect of eliminating China's maritime trade and created a vacuum that European nations, such as Portugal, Spain, and the Netherlands, filled. After Taiwan was conquered by the Manchus in 1683, foreign trade was allowed, but emigration was ruled out on the grounds that Overseas Chinese colonies would become bases of sedition against the government. Granting trade to foreigners was viewed as a way of controlling and manipulating them.

The last form of isolationism that the Chinese were able to impose was the Cohong system, a guild of Chinese merchants assigned by the Chinese government to regulate foreign trade. In 1757 Canton was declared the sole legal port for foreign trade, which was handled exclusively by a small group (originally sixteen) of Chinese merchants. (See map 2.) While the potential profits of the members of the Cohong were great, so were the risks, because they were responsible for the behavior of the foreigners. Direct contact between the foreign traders and the Chinese government was forbidden and all communications had to be funneled through the Cohong. This Cohong system lasted until the Opium War (1839–1842) when the Chinese suffered the first in a series of disastrous defeats and unequal treaties, but this carries us beyond our concluding date of 1800.

European involvement in foreign trade was quite different. In the early 1500s Europeans aspired to greatness but, unlike the Chinese, had not yet attained it.

In 1494 Spain and Portugal had agreed to a proposal initiated by Pope Alexander VI and ratified in the Treaty of Tordesillas that divided the world evenly between these two countries, with a boundary line running down the middle of the North Atlantic Ocean and bisecting South America. Everything to the east of the line, including the Portuguese colony of Brazil, would fall within Portugal's jurisdiction, and everything to the west of that line, including the rest of South and North America, would belong to Spain. In the Pacific Ocean, this boundary was regarded as falling just to the west of the Philippines. This allowed the Portuguese to control the trade routes eastward to Asia and Africa while the Spanish controlled the westward trade routes to the Americas and onward to the Pacific Ocean and the Philippines. (See map 1.)

Portugal's official secrecy clouded accounts of its first contacts with China. The first recorded Portuguese visit to China was in 1514 and the first official Portuguese embassy was led by Tomé Pires from Malacca to Canton in 1517. The Chinese authorities in Canton permitted Pires to proceed to the capital in Beijing, where the envoy waited in vain from July 1520 to February 1521 for an audience with the emperor. Meanwhile the misbehavior of Portuguese traders and sailors in south China—along with accusations that the Portuguese were unscrupulous traders—poisoned the atmosphere. Pires never did meet with the emperor and when the Zhengde Emperor died in May of 1521, Pires and his entourage were ordered back to Canton, where they were imprisoned and their gifts for the emperor confiscated. The envoy and his staff died in prison, but not before sending out letters in 1524 that urged the Portuguese king to mount a military expedition against China. Fortunately this campaign was never initiated, for it would have amounted to a mouse attacking a lion. (At this time, the population of Portugal was approximately one million and that of China over one hundred million.) Instead, the Portuguese more reasonably persisted in their efforts to trade through south China ports and circa 1555 established a trading settlement at Macau (see figure 1.1). The Portuguese colony of Macau has survived for nearly 450 years and is scheduled to be absorbed by China on 20 December 1999.

For three centuries, between 1500 and 1800, Europe and China had extensive contact, which exerted enormous influence. In this book, the term "West" is used synonymously with "Europe" not simply because this usage has become customary but also because the Chinese themselves during the period 1500–1800 commonly referred to Europe as the "Far West" *(Yuan Xi* or *Tai Xi)* and "Western Land" *(Xi du).* They also referred to Europe as the "Western Sea" *(Xi Hai)* in contrast to the "Eastern Sea," or China. Europeans were called "Western people" *(Xi ren),* and European missionaries were called "Western scholars" *(Xi ru),* as opposed to "Chinese scholars" *(Zhong ru).*

During this period, the flow of influence between East and West was not constant. Rather, it ebbed and flowed. And while the influence was never equal in

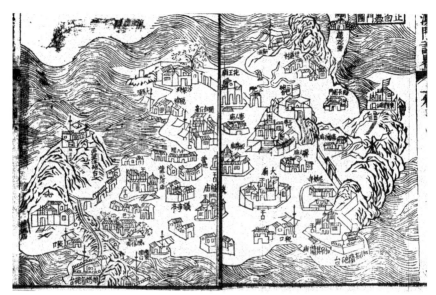

Fig. 1.1. A panoramic drawing of the Portuguese colony Macau, from the *Aomen jilüe, juan* 1, 1800 edition. St. Paul's Church is depicted at the center, slightly to the right above seven wide steps. A recent photograph of the façade and steps of St. Paul's Church is found in figure 3.5.

both directions, there was always at least some influence flowing in both directions so that the movement was never entirely one-way. Similar dynamics of cultural borrowing and assimilation were apparent in both directions. The European Enlightenment's use of Confucianism to support its goal of replacing Christianity with natural religion found its parallel in China in the literati's use of Christianity in an attempt to remove Buddhist and Daoist influences from Confucian teaching. Whereas the three centuries 1500–1800 saw a stronger flow of influence from China to Europe, the following two centuries (1800–1997) were dominated by the flow of influence from the Western world of Europe and North America to China. From 1500 to 1800, missionaries to China carrying Christianity and Western learning met with small degrees of receptivity that were overshadowed by a larger rejection. Likewise, European admiration for China during these years gradually evolved into disillusionment.

We use the patterns that we see in history to make sense of the past. These patterns tend to be a mixture of what is objectively present in history and what we subjectively project into the past. This is a dynamic tension because as history unfolds, the relationship between the present and the past changes. The topics of the four main chapters of this book illustrate this tension as they explore (1) the Chinese acceptance of Western culture and Christianity, (2) the Chinese rejection of these elements, (3) the Western acceptance of Chinese culture and Confucianism, and (4) the Western rejection of these elements. These chapter divisions have a symmetry whose neatness cannot be fully justified in fact. Nevertheless, the symmetry is essentially correct because this was a very two-sided encounter between two cultures with approximately equal claims to greatness. I do not imply by this that greatness is an entirely relative standard to which all cultures can lay equal claim. The greatness of Chinese and European cultures was demonstrated by their ability to influence large areas of the world.

In Europe, the predominant view of the Chinese was captured in images that changed radically between the periods 1500–1800 and 1800–1997. The dates of these cycles are approximate. The first Europeans (the Portuguese) to make contact with the Chinese during this period did so in the early 1500s. This first cycle probably ended with British ambassador Earl Macartney's famous embassy to the court of the Qianlong Emperor in 1793 and the death of the Qianlong Emperor in 1799. The second cycle could be marked as ending at midnight 30 June 1997 with the transfer of the British crown colony of Hong Kong to China. The significance of this event far exceeded the ceremonial symbolism of the British royal yacht *Britannia* sailing out of Hong Kong harbor with Crown Prince Charles aboard. It was one of those events in history that crystallize movements that had been developing incrementally for years. The transfer of Hong Kong to China both symbolized and confirmed China's return to its previously long-standing historical status as the dominant power in East Asia and a leading nation in the world.

During the period 1500–1800, the predominant image of China was captured in the sagely Confucius (551–479 B.C.). The most famous depiction of the learned philosopher shows him standing amid a library filled with books. The image was first published in *Confucius Sinarum Philosophus (Confucius, Philosopher of the Chinese)* in Paris in 1687 and then reduplicated in slightly variant forms in European publications of that time (see figure 1.2). By contrast, one of the most common images of the period 1800–1997 was the hostile depiction of John Chinaman, a vicious-looking pigtailed Chinese male with long nails, whose stereotypical image as a domestic cook led him in one striking illustration to be shown standing over a teapot containing Europeans (see figure 1.3). (Actually, long nails in China were the province of the upper classes rather than domestics.) The implications of uncivilized cannibalism could not have made a greater contrast with the earlier image of a very civilized Confucius. There is no doubt that both images were distortions, one an idealization, the other a pejorative stereotype, and yet both accurately reflected images of the Chinese that Europeans held at different times.

The period 1800–1997 was marked by increased borrowing from the West. This borrowing distorted the dominant American scholarly view of China that,

Fig. 1.2. Confucius depicted as a scholar-sage, from the Jesuit publication *Confucius Sinarum Philosophus* (Paris, 1687). Courtesy of the Niedersächsische Landesbibliothek Hannover. This image was widely reproduced in Europe and epitomized the seventeenth- and eighteenth-century positive view of the Chinese.

in the years following World War II (1945–ca. 1975), saw Sino-Western relations of the period from 1800 onward in terms of Western impact and Chinese response. Post-1800 China was seen as a static culture that had lost its pre-1800 dynamism and was merely responding to external forces, mainly from the West, rather than initiating developments internally. More recent Sinological scholar-

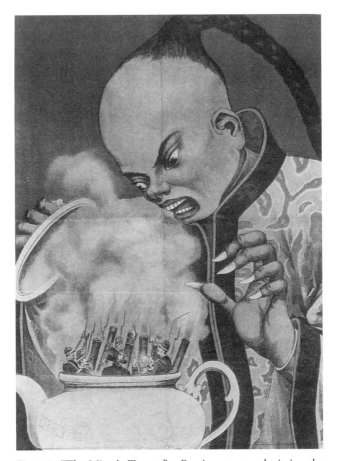

Fig. 1.3. "The Miracle Teapot," a Russian cartoon depicting the Chinese around 1901. Source unknown. The six soldiers in the teapot appear to represent the primary nations that contributed troops to the international force sent in 1900 to lift the Boxer siege of the foreign legations in Beijing. They are (left to right) the United States (?), France, Russia (wearing the distinctive Russian shapka), Japan, Germany, and England. However, Italy and Austria also contributed small contingents. This caustic image shows how negative the Western view of the Chinese had become in the nineteenth and twentieth centuries.

ship has disproved this view and shown that there were dynamic forces in China during the years 1800–1997.

Until the Communists' "Liberation" of China in 1949, much of the borrowing from the West was widespread and experimental. After 1949, the borrowing was limited to the communist theories of Karl Marx, though even these were modified to fit the needs of a unique nonindustrialized land. After 1949 the

Western world's image of China changed in content but was no more positive. John Chinaman was replaced by hordes of Communists, epitomized as an army either of blue ants or of Red Guards, who practiced an oppressive totalitarianism. Except for a few apologists of the political Left in the West, the Chinese Communists were feared but not admired.

The question of whether history repeats itself has been long debated and never conclusively answered. But even if history does not repeat itself in a comprehensive way, we tend to see recurring patterns in the past and we draw meaning from them. Recent years have witnessed a major shift in how the Western world sees China. This new view is characterized by mutual respect rather than an attitude of superiority. To find a similar degree of respect for China in Western history, we must go back to the period 1500–1800. Ironically, what is further removed from the present (1500–1800) may contain more meaning and relevance than the more recent past (1800–1997). That is the subject of this book.

Works Consulted

Chan, Albert. *The Glory and Fall of the Ming Dynasty.* Norman: University of Oklahoma Press, 1982.

Clyde, Paul H., and Burton F. Beers. *The Far East: A History of the Western Impact and the Eastern Response, 1830–1970.* Englewood Cliffs, N.J.: Prentice-Hall, 1971.

Dawson, Raymond. *The Chinese Chameleon: An Analysis of European Conceptions of Chinese Civilization.* London: Oxford University Press, 1967.

Elvin, Mark. *The Pattern of the Chinese Past: A Social and Economic Interpretation.* Stanford, Calif.: Stanford University Press, 1973.

Fairbank, John K., ed. *The Chinese World Order: Traditional China's Foreign Relations.* Cambridge: Harvard University Press, 1968.

Fitzgerald, C. P. *The Chinese View of Their Place in the World.* London: Oxford University Press, 1964.

Franke, Wolfgang. *China and the West: The Cultural Encounter, Thirteenth to Twentieth Centuries.* Translated by R. A. Wilson. New York: Harper & Row, 1967.

Mackerras, Colin. *Western Images of China.* Hong Kong: Oxford University Press, 1991.

Mungello, D. E. "The First Great Cultural Encounter between China and Europe (ca. 1582–ca. 1793)." *Review of Culture* (Macau), 2d ser. (English ed.). 21 (1994): 111–20.

Pan, Lynn. *Sons of the Yellow Emperor: A History of the Chinese Diaspora.* New York: Kodansha, 1994.

Teng, Ssu-yü, and John K. Fairbank, eds. *China's Response to the West: A Documentary Survey, 1839–1923.* Cambridge: Harvard University Press, 1954.

Tsien, Tsuen-hsuin. "Western Impact on China through Translation." *Far Eastern Quarterly* 18 (1954): 305–27.

Wills, John E., Jr. *Pepper, Guns, and Parleys: The Dutch East India Company and China, 1622–1681.* Cambridge: Harvard University Press, 1974.

2

Chinese Acceptance of Western Culture and Christianity

Jesuit Accommodation

While Europeans had appeared in China as early as the thirteenth century in the form of Franciscan missionaries and traders such as Marco Polo, their numbers were too small and the communications between China and Europe were too insubstantial to constitute a genuine cultural encounter. The first substantive encounter between China and the West began when the Portuguese entered south China in the early 1500s. The mere physical presence of foreigners will not guarantee such an encounter. A culture must get beyond the physically defensive reaction of driving the aliens away or the mentally defensive act of closing one's mind to strange ideas. A cultural encounter requires some degree of interaction. Frequent reference to the fabled insularity of the Chinese has obscured the fact that many Chinese did indeed respond to the information and teachings that these Europeans (mainly Christian missionaries) brought to China. Two important questions to answer are: why were Chinese interested in Western learning? and why did Chinese become Christians? Even though the total number of Chinese who participated in the encounter was small, the participants included some of the most creative thinkers of that time. To answer these questions, we must begin with those who brought Western learning and Christianity to China.

One of the results of the Protestant Reformation was that it stimulated a religious revival in the Counter-Reformation that led Catholic missionaries to dominate the Christian mission in China throughout the period 1500–1800. In fact, the London Missionary Society was not founded until 1795 and the first Protestant missionary, Robert Morrison, did not arrive in Chinese territory (Macau) until 1807. Whereas the Protestant Reformation (Lutheranism, Calvinism, Anabaptism) dealt extensively with reforming religious teachings, Protestants were very slow to send missionaries to far-flung regions of the world, such as China. Dutch Calvinists sought their personal fortune in trading with East Asia in the seventeenth and eighteenth centuries but made little attempt to mission-ize the people there. By contrast, although the Catholics refused to change their theology to accommodate the Protestants, they were inspired by the Protestant challenge to reform their hearts and practices. Whereas the Calvinist notion of a predestined elect seems to have discouraged missionary work, the Jesuit empha-sis on free will in matters of salvation had the opposite effect.

In the enthusiasm generated by the Counter-Reformation and to compensate for losses to Protestantism in Europe, dedicated Catholic missionaries were sent on the newly established trade routes throughout the world. Some of the most prominent of these missionaries included members of a new religious order, the Society of Jesus, that had been instituted in 1540 to assist the pope in counter-ing the Protestant challenge. In fact, the members of this society, called Jesuits, dominated the Christian mission in China during the years 1500–1800. While a number of Catholic groups (Franciscans, Dominicans, Augustinians, Jesuits, the Society of Foreign Missions of Paris, the Congregation for the Propagation of the Faith, and others) sent missionaries to China, the names of Jesuits became most famous. The fame of these Jesuits has distorted our understanding of the history of Christianity in China because historians have overemphasized the role that the Jesuits played and slighted the role of other Catholic orders.

The founder of the Jesuit China mission was Francis Xavier (1506–1552), a Spaniard who visited Japan and the East Indies and who wished to enter China. Although he never penetrated the Chinese mainland and died on the offshore island of Shangchuan in 1552, his efforts were an inspiration to later Jesuits. Of these Jesuits, none is more famous than the Italian Father Matteo Ricci, S.J. (1552–1610), who is widely known to the Chinese as Li Madou. Perhaps the most brilliant of a group of Jesuits characterized by brilliance, Ricci arrived in Macau in 1582 as one of the founders of the modern mission.

A gifted linguist, Ricci used the mnemonic techniques of Europe to impress the Chinese literati with their potential as a tool to memorize the Confucian clas-sics. The practical value of such a tool in China cannot be overemphasized since nearly all paths to status and success lay through passing the civil service exami-nations that were based on memorizing the classics. Ricci also used European cartography to appeal to the literati by producing a world map with all the place names given in Chinese. This famous map caused quite a stir in China. Its use of Jesuit accommodation was shown in placing China near the center of the map, thereby accommodating the Chinese view of their country as the Middle Kingdom (*Zhongguo*). In 1601, after nineteen years of effort (including the clever use of European curiosity pieces, such as a self-striking clock and a harp-sichord), Ricci had attained the remarkable achievement of securing permission from the imperial government to establish a missionary residence in the capital of Beijing.

Although not the first Jesuit to enter China, Ricci was a pioneer in formulating the Jesuit missionary approach to China. Jesuit accommodation was developed to meet the unique demands of the mission field in China. Although Jesuit missionary policy as a whole stressed the accommodation of Christianity to indigenous elements of a foreign culture, nowhere had European missionaries encountered such an advanced culture as in China. This forced them to make difficult choices about what to accept and what to reject. If they accepted elements of Chinese culture that contradicted the Christian faith, the accommodation would become theologically invalid. If, on the other hand, they did not accept certain essential elements in Chinese culture, then the Chinese would reject Christianity as foreign and alien. If Christianity was to thrive in China, it would have to be inculturated there. This means that it would no longer be seen as an exotic, foreign religion and instead would become not only something familiar but also a force that transformed Chinese culture.

The Chinese response to Christianity was clearly divisible along class lines, between the literati and the common people. The literati received the most respect and prestige of any group in traditional Chinese society. Their status was based, at least in theory and to a large extent in reality, upon the egalitarian principle of education. Intensive study of the Confucian classics was aimed at preparing one for the official examinations. Success in the examinations on three ascending levels—somewhat comparable to the bachelor's, master's, and doctoral degrees—brought the immediate rewards of social prestige and certain legal privileges, such as exemption from physical abuse at the hands of scholar-officials. (The Chinese legal system contained no presumption of innocence of an accused individual, and corporal punishment was commonly used to extract confessions.)

In the long run, success in the examinations brought social prestige and official appointment that enabled one to participate in networks of enormous political and social influence and to obtain financial rewards from holding office. These financial rewards were usually invested in farmland—oftentimes managed by a clan (extended family)—that provided a financial return as well as refuge in the event of dismissal from office. As a result, there was considerable overlap between scholar-officials and landowning gentry.

In the period 1500–1800 these scholar-officials identified with the teachings of Confucius. Although they might participate in Buddhist and Daoist practices, such as using Buddhist monks for funerals, Confucianism became the philosophy associated with wealth and power. The poor, by contrast, were more likely to find refuge in Buddhism and Daoism. The poor were even more closely associated with socially destitute groups, such as secret societies, that blended Buddhist, Daoist, and other popular religious elements with illegal activities to scrape out a bare subsistence.

When the Jesuits first attempted to establish a residence in south China, they adopted the robes of the Buddhist monks, but these missionaries soon realized their error and chose Confucianism rather than Buddhism as the basis for accommodation. This choice was understandable, given the cultural and social affinities of the highly educated Jesuits (many of whom also came from prominent families in Europe) with the highly educated and socially prestigious Chinese literati. Buddhist monks, who had declined in ability and social status from earlier periods, were criticized by the Jesuits for their intellectual superstitions, immoral practices, and social coarseness, while the literati were praised for their refinement and emphasis on learning. In addition, the literati presented a highly attractive power base to the Jesuits, who were accustomed in Europe and elsewhere to working close to the apex of the power structure. Moreover, a degree of tacit acceptance by the scholar-officials was necessary if the Jesuits were to remain in China.

Jesuit Conversions of the Literati

In the early years of the mission, particularly in the more open intellectual atmosphere of the late Ming, the Jesuits achieved some success in converting prominent scholar-officials. This success came through the conscious attempt at blending Confucianism with Christianity while criticizing Buddhism and Daoism. This attempt had first been formulated by Ricci and other Jesuit pioneers in China and was continued by the Jesuits throughout most of the seventeenth century. The most prominent of this first generation of converts were Xu Guangqi (1562–1633), Li Zhizao (1565–1630), and Yang Tingyun (1557–1627). (See figure 2.1.) These three were regarded as the Three Pillars of the early Christian church. Xu was a first grand secretary, perhaps the highest official position in the Ming dynasty, and Li and Yang also occupied important positions.

Although the Three Pillars were all eminent scholar-officials who had studied the Confucian classics in order to pass the official examinations, their individual paths to Christianity differed. Xu was the first to be baptized (1601 in Nanjing), followed by Li Zhizao (1610 in Beijing) and Yang Tingyun (1611 in Hangzhou). All three remained committed to Confucian values, although Li was critical of Neo-Confucianism. Prior to their baptisms, their interest in Buddhism had varied; Yang was probably the most interested. After their baptisms, all three became harsh critics of Buddhism. Intellectually, all three harmonized Christianity with Confucianism.

However, a religious conversion is not a purely intellectual experience, and at least two of the Three Pillars underwent religious experiences that were crucial to their decision to be baptized. The personal crisis of failing the highest level of examination (the doctoral level or *jinshi* exam) in 1597 made Xu

Fig. 2.1. An original color portrait of the eminent Christian scholar-official Xu Guangqi (1562–1633), now preserved in the Shanghai Council for the Protection of Historical Relics (Shanghai Shi Wenwu Baoguan Weiyuanhui). The crane on Xu's jacket is an insignia of high scholar-official rank.

Guangqi receptive to receiving instruction from the Jesuit fathers in 1598. This failure also probably saved him from taking a concubine, which was part of the standard celebratory practices of having arrived at this elevated status. In 1600, shortly after meeting Ricci, Xu had a dream of a temple with three chapels. The first chapel contained a shrine to God, the second a shrine to the son, and the third was empty. Much later Xu realized that this was a dream of the Trinity (Father, Son, and Holy Spirit). After failing the *jinshi* examination for a second time, Xu was deeply moved by a painting of the Madonna and child and shortly thereafter was baptized.

Although Li Zhizao was much influenced by the mathematics and astronomy that Ricci taught, he was even more influenced by Ricci's character. Li had the closest relationship to Ricci of any of the Three Pillars, but his reluctance to send away his concubine was the final obstacle to his baptism. Finally, he experienced the personal crisis of a very serious illness in Beijing in early 1610 in which, unattended by relatives, he was personally nursed for weeks by Ricci. At what appeared to be the point of death, he accepted the Christian faith and was baptized by Ricci. Li recovered soon thereafter; Ricci died in May of that year. In 1611 Li resigned from official duty and returned to his home in Hangzhou to care for his father, who was ill, inviting the Jesuit fathers Lazzaro Cattaneo (1560–1640) and Nicolas Trigault (1577–1628) to accompany him.

Yang Tingyun's conversion was much less influenced by Ricci than was Li's. Yang met Ricci in Beijing, possibly in 1602, but did not become seriously interested in Christianity until almost a decade later. In 1609 he resigned his official post and retired to his home of Hangzhou. When he visited Li's home to express his condolences on the death of Li's father, he met Fathers Cattaneo and Trigault. He began serious discussions with them about Christianity and, after a long internal struggle, became a Christian. He first had to resolve serious questions about the veneration of the Buddha, the Incarnation of God in Jesus, and Christian redemption. Finally, he had to take the extremely difficult step of sending his concubine, who had given him two sons, to a separate dwelling. At one point, he was moved by a pictorial image of Christ. Although it is difficult to know the exact motive that led Yang to be baptized, it is clear that he differed from Xu and Li in not being drawn to Christianity because of either a personal crisis or admiration for Western science and mathematics.

The culture of the late Ming dynasty that the Christian missionaries encountered in China was experimental and had a looser sense of Confucian orthodoxy than other periods of Chinese history. Many late-Ming literati were radical in their willingness to synthesize various teachings into a harmonious unity. The willingness of Ming culture to minimize differences and emphasize similarities was revealed in works like the famous novel *Journey to the West (Xi yu ji)*—also known as *Monkey*—by Wu Cheng'en (ca. 1500–1582). In this novel and throughout Ming culture, the teachings of Confucianism, Buddhism, and Daoism were blended in syncretic unity under the often quoted phrase "the Three Teachings are really one." Such a blending would have been unthinkable in other periods of Chinese history, when the exponents of these respective teachings competed and clashed with one another in their search for truth and imperial favor.

While the Jesuits refused to accept the blending of these three particular teachings, they did use the syncretic spirit of the Ming. However, instead of blending Buddhism and Daoism with Confucianism, the Jesuits sought to blend Christianity with Confucianism. They did this by attempting to displace Buddhism and Daoism with Christianity and to create a Confucian-Christian synthesis. The eminent convert Xu Guangqi helped to shape this approach and expressed it with the famous phrase that Christianity should "supplement Confucianism and displace Buddhism" *(bu Ru yi Fo)*. While Confucianism was essentially a moral and social teaching that spoke only implicitly of spiritual forces, Buddhism spoke specifically and in great detail on spiritual matters. Confucianism's relative silence on spirits made it less vulnerable to criticism as a pagan religion, and its emphasis on moral and spiritual cultivation was viewed as reconcilable with Christianity's explicit treatment of spiritual forces and one God. Furthermore, elements like the Chinese emphasis on filial piety were very much in accord with the biblical command to honor one's parents, and Confucius's formulation of the Golden Rule was very similar to what Jesus expressed in Matthew 7:12.

Later literati converts, such as Shang Huqing (ca. 1619–after 1698) of Jinan in Shandong province and Zhang Xingyao (1633–after 1715) of Hangzhou, were less prominent. Shang and Zhang were thoughtful men who carried to deeper levels the attempt to reconcile Confucianism with Christianity. Furthermore, Shang and Zhang, in typical literati fashion, saw themselves in a tradition of Confucian-Christian literati in which Xu Guangqi had been an earlier master. They both advanced Xu's formula, "supplement Confucianism and displace Buddhism." Shang had the unique experience of collaborating with both a Jesuit and a Franciscan in Jinan, in spite of the more typical hostility between Jesuit and non-Jesuit missionaries in China. During the years 1660–1664, Shang collaborated with Father Antonio Caballero a Santa Maria, O.F.M. (1602–1669) to produce several works in Chinese on Christianity. Typical of these was *Confucianism and Christianity Compared (Tian Ru yin)*, in which passages from the Confucian Four Books were cited to show the similarities between the two teachings. Shang also wrote a lengthy manuscript entitled "A Warning on the Need to Supplement Confucianism" *(Bu Ru wengao)* (1664), which was never published. Several statements from this work reveal how unchauvinistic Shang's outlook was: for example, "People of the Eastern Sea [China] and Western Sea [Europe] live in different lands but under the same Heaven. They speak different languages but live by the same principles."

In 1702, after extensive study of Chinese history and the Confucian classics, Zhang Xingyao refined Xu's formula of supplementing Confucianism and displacing Buddhism into a three-part formula (harmonize, supplement, and transcend) to explain the similarities and differences between Confucianism and Christianity. In the first part, Zhang assembled numerous quotations from the ancient Chinese classics to show that Christianity and Confucianism were in agreement. In the second part, Christianity supplemented Confucianism in spiritual and moral cultivation as well as in other areas. In the third part, Christian revelation transcended the teaching of Confucianism. Zhang, too, voiced remarkably unchauvinistic sentiments. In the preface to a work entitled *Clearly*

Distinguishing the Heavenly Teaching [i.e., Christianity] [from Heterodoxy] he wrote: "In the Eastern Sea and the Western Sea sages arise who are identical in thinking." What is even more significant about this statement is that Zhang was quoting from the famous Neo-Confucian philosopher Lu Xiangshan (1139–1193). This indicates that Zhang saw himself not as an original thinker but rather after the model of Confucius, a transmitter of the wisdom of antiquity. Clearly, Zhang saw his acceptance of Christianity as within the orthodox tradition of Confucianism, even if he appeared to be a voice in the wilderness.

The development of these insights was the result of extensive collaboration between the missionaries and the literati who were sympathetic to Christianity. The Jesuits tended to write collaboratively in a way that obscured individual authorship. Furthermore, the Jesuits were often hesitant to identify the role of Chinese collaborators because of hostile critics who would have jumped on such identifications as evidence of heterodox sources in Jesuit writings. Consequently, it is often very difficult to identify specific Jesuits and, even more so, Chinese literati who contributed to a particular work.

The Jesuit approach in missionizing was to work from the top down in converting social classes. In China, the highly educated Jesuits—the Society of Jesus is unsurpassed among Catholic religious orders in the effort it spends in educating its members—found their social and intellectual counterparts in the Confucian literati. Consequently, Ricci had a rapport with Xu Guangqi that enabled them to work closely together. However, after the Manchu conquest of the native Chinese dynasty in 1644 and the founding of the Qing dynasty, the cultural atmosphere in China became less open to foreign influences, and the status of the literati converted by the Jesuits dropped to those with lesser degrees and prestige, such as Shang Huqing and Zhang Xingyao. The success of missionizing a nation from the top down depended upon obtaining conversions among the most powerful and influential people so that they could influence lesser individuals to follow their example. As the status of the literati converts dropped, the Jesuit effort began to falter. But the process of assimilating Christianity in China did not stop. It continued to ebb and flow down through the years, undergoing a gradual shift from European to (after 1949) Chinese leadership.

Missionary Antagonism with Chinese Society

There were missionaries of other religious orders in China who aimed their work at a constituency very different from that of the Jesuits. Franciscans, particularly Spaniards, came from a culture that had been deeply influenced by the *Reconquista* by which Muslims and Jews in Spain had been forcibly converted to Christianity or expelled. Rather than seek accommodation as did the Jesuits, the

Franciscans were stimulated by opposition. The Franciscan missionaries in China were energized by seeing their community of Christians as an island of believers surrounded by a sea of hostility. Inspired by the model of Saint Francis of Assisi, the Franciscan missionaries in China emphasized submission and martyrdom, both in their own training and in their apostolate.

The Franciscans aimed their missionizing at less prestigious groups in China. Writing in 1656, Father Caballero stated that his conversions in Shandong province (see map 2) had been entirely limited to the humblest and poorest people. He had failed to convert a single member of the literati during the preceding six years. Caballero expressed his frustration in dealing with wealthy people and merchants who showed little interest in religion. And yet, during his fifteen-year apostolate (1650–1665) in Shandong, Caballero baptized five thousand of these humble people. While the Franciscan missionaries did not ignore the need to cultivate the scholar-officials for political purposes, nearly all of their baptisms were among the lower social orders. The social and class antagonism in China at that time was expressed by the upper classes (literati) often being anti-Buddhist and anti-Daoist and by the lower classes (shopkeepers, craftsmen, peasants, workers, and the dispossessed) being anti-Confucian. Consequently, religious and class antagonism came together to reinforce one another in a way that would foster conflict with the Chinese government.

Because of the hostility that surrounded the Christians, the Franciscans resorted to secret meetings of their followers as a necessary expedient in circumventing the official prohibitions against their teachings. (One notes parallels to an underground Christian church—with an unofficial Catholic hierarchy and unregistered Protestant house churches— in contemporary China.) Secret meetings by Christian lay groups, such as the Confraternity of the Passion, may have been necessary, but they were also dangerous because they reinforced a link between Christianity and heretical, subversive societies, such as the White Lotus Society. The White Lotus Society was actually a group of loosely organized peasant secret societies that shared a quasi-Buddhist religious structure. Secret societies have a nearly two-thousand-year history in China. They are linked to peasant uprisings, for which the societies provided an organization and ideology. The peasant uprisings were nearly always aimed at the scholar-gentry class, who were viewed by the peasants as their oppressors because they controlled both the land and the government bureaucracy. Because of this intense hostility, the secret societies were viewed with suspicion and enmity by the scholar-officials. Like the secret societies, Christianity was often accused by the literati of subversive practices, such as prohibiting ancestor worship, meeting in small groups, using magical techniques to control followers, and deceiving the people.

These criticisms were not based on mere suspicion. After the lapse of conversions of eminent figures, Christianity found its greatest following among the same lower social classes who joined the secret societies. Not only did Christianity and the White Lotus Teaching draw many of their followers from the same lower classes but also some individuals claimed to be adherents of both teachings at the same time. Certain White Lotus adherents in Shandong around 1700 even called their teaching by the same name as Christianity, namely, "Lord of Heaven Teaching" *(Tianzhujiao).* This ambiguity may have been intentional. By claiming to be Christians, the members of the White Lotus sect were able to circumvent the governmental prohibition against their sect and obtain the less restrictive prohibitions applied to Christianity. (Christianity had been awarded greater freedom by the Kangxi Emperor's Toleration Edict of 1692 and by other favorable imperial rulings obtained largely as rewards to the Jesuits for their service to the throne.) The anti-Confucian attitudes of the lower classes, along with their tendency to indiscriminately mix with members of quasi-Buddhist and quasi-Daoist secret societies, made them an object of official repression that would spill over to Chinese Christians.

Once the Jesuits had chosen to concentrate on converting the Chinese literati as the first step toward converting the entire society, elements associated with the literati assumed crucial importance. These elements included the choice of a Chinese name for the Christian God and how to regard the rites performed to honor Confucius and familial ancestors. Was it permissible, these early Jesuits wondered, to use ancient Chinese terms such as *Shangdi* (Lord-on-High) or *Tian* (Heaven) to refer to God? Or were these terms too tainted with pagan associations in the minds of the Chinese to convey Christian concepts accurately? If so, was it then possible to coin a new Chinese word, *Tianzhu* (Lord of Heaven), or was it necessary to develop a Chinese transliteration for the name of God, such as *De-u-se* for Latin *Deus* (God)?

In regard to the crucial matter of rites, were the Chinese rites dedicated to Confucius and to ancestors acts of worship? Or were they essentially acts of social honor and civil respect? These issues, which became part of the Chinese Rites Controversy, went to the very heart of the missionary effort because they required Europeans to separate what was truly essential to the Christian faith from what was merely cultural and secondary. The battles were fought more by Europeans than by Chinese, because these issues challenged European traditions more than Chinese traditions. The challenges that Christianity posed to Chinese converts involved more of an attempt to reconcile with the Confucian tradition Christian ideas such as the Creation, Incarnation (of God in the human form of Jesus), Crucifixion, and Resurrection.

Jesuit accommodation, with its inherent sympathy and respect for Chinese culture, tended to tolerate many indigenous Chinese cultural elements in deciding these questions, but this produced a negative reaction among many European Christians. Even some Sinologists have questioned whether the Jesuits' synthesis went so far in accommodating Confucianism that what resulted was a diluted form of Christianity, which the Dutch Sinologist E. Zürcher has called "Confucian monotheism." Although few Jesuits expressed dissent to accommodation, many non-Jesuit missionaries in China and European critics of the Jesuits did. The resulting Rites Controversy debate did great damage to the Christian mission in China but may have been an inevitable part of the cultural encounter.

Even with this degree of accommodation, the Jesuits faced enormous resistance to Christianity from the Chinese. The concept of a heavenly God had a close counterpart in Confucianism. The notion of an afterlife with experiences in Heaven and Hell had already been introduced into China by Buddhism, although not all literati accepted these concepts. The Creation and the Incarnation of God on Earth in the form of Jesus were new ideas in China, but even they did not face the greatest resistance. It was the Crucifixion of Christ and the Resurrection that the literati most resisted. In a society like the Chinese, which made sharp social distinctions on the basis of whether one worked with one's hands or one's mind, the literati earned exemption from most forms of corporal punishment. Because physical violence was associated with the lower, vulgar classes of society, it was very difficult for the literati to accept that the human being who was the incarnation of God would submit to such a degrading punishment.

Because of the negative reaction of literati to the Crucifixion and Resurrection, Ricci and later Jesuits delayed presenting these fundamental teachings in the religious instruction to prospective converts. Other groups of missionaries, such as the Franciscans, whose apostolate was primarily among the lower classes, taught the Crucifixion and Resurrection more openly. The Jesuits could scarcely display the crucifix, because it was perceived as a form of black magic aimed at the person of the Chinese emperor and consequently evoked intense hostility. Nevertheless, the Jesuits did teach the Crucifixion and Resurrection, and this is clearly shown by Father Aleni's adaptation of Nadal's famous illustrated life of Christ discussed below and depicted in figure 2.4. However, because of its sensitivity, the Jesuits tended to reserve the Crucifixion as one of the last teachings to be imparted to converts.

Ricci's attitude toward Chinese culture and society was a relatively balanced mixture of praise and criticism. He admired the enormous size of China and its populace, the diversity of its crops, its favorable climate, the industry of its people, and its Confucian morality. But he was especially critical of Buddhist and Daoist monks whose personal and sexual immorality was flagrant. He was highly critical of Chinese sensuality and slavery, which he felt were related. And he reserved some of his harshest criticisms for homosexual practices, particularly sodomy, which he regarded as widely practiced among Chinese males. The harshness of Ricci's comments needs to be viewed in light of the Counter-Reformation's active campaigns against homosexuality that had been conducted by the

Roman Inquisition under Pope Paul IV (r. 1555–1559) during Ricci's child-hood.

It is difficult to conceive of the Italian Ricci advocating such a harsh punish-ment as that carried out by the Spaniards in Manila who burned several Chinese males for homosexual acts in the 1580s. Rather, Ricci's comments reveal an anti-homosexual attitude that was shared by many Europeans at the time of the Counter-Reformation, in spite of the fact that homosexual practices like sodomy had been widespread in Italian cities such as Florence, Rome, and Venice. The extent of these practices reflects the fact that sodomy was practiced not by a sub-group of "homosexuals" (for which no word yet existed) but rather between young men and boys as a phase preceding a heterosexual adulthood, which com-monly began with marriage around thirty years of age. In the period prior to the Counter-Reformation, sodomy had been regarded as a misdemeanor rather than a mortal sin and transgressors were usually lightly punished. However, during the Counter-Reformation, attitudes toward homosexuality became much harsher, and Ricci's criticism of homosexual practices among Chinese males reflected this hardening of attitudes in Europe.

The homophobia of the Counter-Reformation caused missionaries like Ricci to exaggerate the extent of homosexual practices in China. There was a male homosexual tradition throughout Chinese history in which anal intercourse was practiced. Active and passive roles in sodomy were determined by age, wealth, employment, and education, duplicating the dominant-inferior roles in other areas of society. This explains why Ricci criticized the Chinese institutionalizing of male prostitution among boys and actors with low social standing. There was no division of men into heterosexual and homosexual categories, and many of these same-sex practices were engaged in by those who also engaged in hetero-sexual practices. Nevertheless, while there was general tolerance of same-sex prac-tices in Chinese history, it is doubtful that they were as widespread in China as Ricci stated. Ricci's perception was probably shaped by his exposure to sophisti-cated urban life among literati in Nanjing and Beijing, where much of the same-sex activity was concentrated.

The Closing of Chinese Minds (ca. 1644)

After the Manchu conquest of 1644, Chinese resistance to foreign influences increased. Such a resistance was not typical of Chinese history. During the seven centuries from A.D. 200 to 900, China had been relatively open to foreigners and foreign influences. This was the age when Buddhism entered China from Cen-tral Asia and was assimilated into Chinese culture. This period culminated with the great age of the Tang dynasty (618–907), which was cosmopolitan, sophisticated, and largely acceptant of non-Han peoples, whether Turks from Central Asia or Muslim Arabs from the Indian Ocean region. Han Chinese represent an ethnic group who share a culture. (Over 90 percent of the 1.3 billion people who live in China today are Han Chinese.) It is difficult to classify Chinese primarily in terms of physical characteristics. We can say that Han Chinese belong to what anthropologists have called the Mongoloid racial group, which includes the distinctive features of straight black hair, dark eyes, flat faces, epicanthoid folds (almond-shaped eyes), and a minimum of facial and body hair. But many non-Han Chinese lack these physical characteristics.

Because of the physical differences between Han and non-Han Chinese, identity as a Chinese has traditionally been regarded as more a matter of culture than race. This shared culture is based upon the written Chinese characters. However, with the founding of the Ming dynasty in 1368, the Chinese began a long, gradual process of turning inward (see chapter 1). This turning inward may have been due to political decisions by early Ming emperors, or it may have been due to the remarkable prosperity of the Ming dynasty. In any case, it strengthened and solidified feelings of Chinese ethnocentrism, which in its extreme forms produced chauvinism (intense feelings of superiority) and xenophobia (antiforeign feeling). Over the period 1500–1800 these feelings gradually increased and intensified. This process explains, in part, why Chinese literati were more receptive to Western influences during the earlier part of this period than the later part.

What is notable is that Chinese feelings of chauvinism and xenophobia lagged behind technological and economic realities by several centuries. China's science and technology peaked sometime in the mid-fourteenth century (approximately when the Ming dynasty was founded), when it became the most populous nation and the one with the highest rate of literacy. Creativity in science and technology began to falter and China entered into a long and very gradual, almost imperceptible decline. It would take several centuries for this loss of intellectual creativity to translate into economic, military, social, and cultural decline. Moreover, the economic prosperity of the Ming served to mask the underlying scientific and technological stagnation. Chinese feelings of cultural superiority became so ingrained that foreigners would recognize the signs of decline before the Chinese themselves did. Lord Macartney of Great Britain, during his embassy to the court of the Qianlong Emperor in 1793, was one of the first foreign observers to notice these signs of drift and lack of forward momentum. Meanwhile the Chinese felt themselves to be living in a great golden age, without realizing that the glory belonged to an Indian summer rather than to summer's peak.

The position of Jesuit accommodation became less tenable after the Manchu invasion of 1644, as the Chinese reverted to a stricter sense of orthodoxy during the Qing dynasty. With the decline of the syncretic spirit in Chinese culture, the literati became less willing to accept the synthesis of Confucianism with a foreign religion. In fact, the literati became reluctant to accept the blending of Confucianism with any non-Confucian elements, including Buddhism and Daoism. There was a reassertion of the transmission of the *Dao* (Way or Truth) from the ancient sages through Confucius and his followers down to the present. There was little place in such a perspective for a foreign religion. This was the cultural current against which Jesuits of the late seventeenth and eighteenth centuries had to struggle, and it made conversions of eminent literati far more difficult than they previously had been.

Although cultural conditions in China became less fertile for Christianity, the Jesuits continued to find employment in prominent positions at the court. However, because they were occupied with the interests of the court, their emphasis shifted away from the cultivation of the literati in the provinces. The continued prominence of the Jesuits during the late seventeenth century and throughout the eighteenth was indicative of the quality of the missionaries sent to China and the willingness of the Manchu emperors to make use of their services. Men like the German Johann Adam Schall von Bell (Tang Ruowang, 1592–1666) and the Belgian Ferdinand Verbiest (Nan Huairen, 1623–1688) would have been outstanding in practically any environment. Fathers Schall and Verbiest were the first Europeans to head the important Chinese Bureau of Astronomy, where the mathematically trained Jesuits held prominent positions for more than 150 years. (See figure 2.2.) When the Manchus conquered China in 1644 and established the Qing dynasty, the technical skills of the Jesuits enabled them to be retained at the Beijing court, smoothing the transition between political masters. Schall and Verbiest were also close to the Manchu emperors of China and had regular contact with them.

Schall established a particularly close relationship with the first Manchu ruler, the young Shunzhi Emperor (r. 1644–1661), who came the closest of any Chinese emperor to being baptized. The emperor was light-skinned with dark hair, somewhat slight, but a good horseman in the Manchu manner. He was bright and studied hard to master the Chinese language. He was a conscientious ruler, decisive, with a strong interest in religion. During the first seven years after taking personal control of the government (1651–1657), he developed an unusually close and affectionate relationship with Schall, consulting him on affairs of state as well as religious matters. The emperor often called Schall to his imperial quarters, sometimes at night, or impulsively visited Schall at the mission residence near the palace. He was very informal with Schall, sitting cross-legged on Schall's bed and asking about Christianity and life in Europe. In fact, he called Schall by the affectionate Manchu name of *ma-fa* (grandpa), an indicator that this relationship between a teenager and a priest in his sixties was much like that

Fig. 2.2. The ancient Beijing Astronomical Observatory of the Bureau of Astronomy, first built under the Mongols and located just inside the southeast portion of the Tartar City Wall. Although the wall has been dismantled, the observatory remains, located on Jiangguomenwai Avenue. The platform containing the astronomical instruments stands over forty-five feet (fourteen meters) in height. The Jesuit Father F. Verbiest took a leading role in the construction of these instruments and in the running of the observatory.

of grandfather and grandson. The emperor was particularly fascinated by an illustrated life of Christ (probably based on Nadal's work) among Schall's books. When he came to the Crucifixion of Christ, he was so moved that he fell to his knees while Schall knelt beside him. The emperor also visited Schall's church and had Schall explain all the eucharistic vestments.

The relationship between Schall and the Shunzhi Emperor was such that Schall could present his petitions directly to the emperor, bypassing the usual official screening process. But although prospects for converting the emperor of China to Christianity looked favorable, the moment passed. The Shunzhi Emperor appears to have been very much interested in sex and disinclined to accept Schall's admonitions about controlling his sex drives or, in Schall's vocabulary, "lusts of the flesh." Moreover, the Jesuits' demand for strict adherence to monogamy conflicted with a Chinese emperor's duty to have an active sex life with multiple wives in order to produce an abundant supply of heirs to the throne. After 1658 the emperor turned increasingly to the more solicitous voices of eunuchs who encouraged him to indulge his desires while they increased their political power. His religious interests continued but they moved in the direction of Chan (Zen) Buddhism. At any rate, the Shunzhi Emperor did not have a long life. Weakened by tuberculosis, he died of smallpox in 1661, one month short of his twenty-third birthday.

While Jesuit influence on the Chinese literati peaked in the late Ming between 1600 and 1644 (the year of the Manchu conquest), Jesuit influence on the Manchu rulers of China peaked in the early Qing dynasty between 1644 and 1705. The Jesuits had converted several prominent scholar-officials who assisted them. One of the most important officials of the Qing period, Wei Yijie (1616–1686), was a secret Christian. Although Jesuits continued to work at the court throughout the eighteenth century, their work as painters and architects appears to have given them a narrower craftsman status, which lowered their access to the throne.

Jesuit influence on the Chinese throne was aided by the missionaries' brilliance, training, and spiritual discipline, but it was hindered by a growing contentiousness. Not only did the Jesuits contend with other Christian missionaries in the Rites Controversy and over other issues, but they also argued with one another. One of the greatest sources of conflict among the Jesuits themselves was based upon nationalistic differences. Out of 920 Jesuits who participated in the China mission between 1552 and 1800, 314, or over one-third, were Portuguese. Considering that Portugal had a population of only about 1 million people at that time, how do we account for this high proportion of Portuguese? In part, it was due to the Portuguese crown's support of Christian missions, and in part, it was due to the *padroado* (a monopoly granted by the papacy over missionary and other activities in Asia).

The division of the world between Spain and Portugal explains why, until the end of the seventeenth century, there were only two official routes from Europe to China. (See map 1.) The shorter route involved obtaining a visa and passage out of Lisbon on Portuguese ships, which went around the southern Cape of Africa and landed at Goa in India. The traveler then obtained onward passage on Portuguese ships to Macau. The longer route involved departure from Seville on Spanish ships. After crossing the Atlantic to Mexico, one crossed Central America to Acapulco and took passage on a Spanish ship across the Pacific Ocean to the Philippines. Onward passage from the Philippines to China was fraught with difficulties because the Portuguese would arrest anyone who disembarked in Macau without a Portuguese visa. Consequently, the Spanish Franciscans tended to avoid Macau and land illegally on the coast of Fujian province in southeastern China.

While Spain produced many China missionaries, most of them were Franciscans and Dominicans rather than Jesuits. There were also many Italian Jesuits (99) who served in China, but Italian identity was diluted by the fact that at that time Italian affiliations were regional rather than national. By the end of the seventeenth century, Dutch and French ships had broken the Portuguese monopoly on shipping routes to East Asia. Although the Dutch Calvinists would send no missionaries to China until after 1800, the large number of French Jesuits (130) reflected the emergence of France as a European power. The French Jesuits, like the French political leaders, were unwilling to honor the Portuguese monopoly, and this led to contention in China between Portuguese Jesuits, including Father Tomé Pereira (1645–1708), who was a favorite of the Kangxi Emperor, and the French Jesuits, who were arriving in increasing numbers. This conflict diminished respect for the missionaries in the eyes of the Chinese.

Chinese Reaction to Christian Paintings and Engravings

When the missionaries arrived in China, they brought works from one of the most magnificent achievements of Western art. Since the Renaissance, pictorial images had played an enormous role in European Christianity and missionaries to China rightly saw them as important tools for teaching the Chinese about Christianity. Consequently, the first European works of art to arrive in China were devotional paintings, illustrated books, and engravings, many of which were devoted to biblical themes. They arrived on Portuguese and Spanish ships traveling from Europe to China.

The devotional oil paintings produced in the Renaissance fascinated the Chinese. Not only did the pictorial images foster conversions among Chinese, but also their lifelike quality caused the merely curious to flock to the Christian churches to view the Western pictures. Chinese were impressed by the Western use of three-dimensional space through the techniques of perspective and chiaroscuro. (Chiaroscuro [pronounced kee-ar-eh skyoor-o] is a style of painting that uses only light and shade to attain a third dimension.) Western engravings and illustrated books also struck a responsive chord among the Chinese and were easily copied by Chinese wood engravers. These books were reproduced as part of the extensive Jesuit effort to translate European books into Chinese. By the end of the eighteenth century, over four hundred such translations had been produced in China.

In 1578 a group of Spanish Franciscans processed through Macau carrying a small print of the Virgin and child after Saint Luke, copied from a work in the Church of Santa Maria Maggiore in Rome. However, when the Jesuits displayed a painting of the Virgin and child at their residence in Zhaoqing near Canton, Chinese confused the Virgin with the Buddhist bodhisattva Guanyin. In Buddhism, a bodhisattva is characterized by compassion for the suffering of other sentient beings. Although enlightened, the bodhisattva delays entry into Nirvana, instead seeking continued rebirth in the world of suffering in order to assist other human beings to attain enlightenment. Because Chinese women often prayed to the compassionate Guanyin for assistance in conceiving and bearing a child, preferably a boy, Guanyin is sometimes portrayed with a son in her arms. To eliminate this confusion, the Jesuits replaced the picture of the Virgin and child with a painting portraying the theme *Salvator Mundi* (Savior of the world), which typically shows the upper body of Christ, who is holding an orb and cross in one hand and blessing it with the other hand. The painting was by Father Giovanni Niccolo (Cola), S.J. (1560–1626) of Naples, who arrived in Macau with Ricci in 1582.

Most of the artwork initially used by missionaries in China had been shipped from Europe. Although some of it had been produced by eminent European artists, it became clear that the iconographic needs of the missionaries could best be supplied by Chinese artists. In Manila, the Jesuit painter Father Antonius Sedeno ran a school for Chinese painters, supplying churches in the Philippines with devotional pictures in the Western style. Of more significance was the school for painters in Japan run by Father Niccolo. A school for copper engravers was established in Japan in the late sixteenth century.

The first Chinese artist to serve the Jesuits was the lay brother Yu Wenhui (alias Manuel Pereira), S.J. (1575–1633). Yu was born in Macau and was sent to study painting in Japan under Father Niccolo in the 1590s. Although his religious paintings were mediocre, Yu assisted Ricci on his deathbed in Beijing in 1610 and later painted the famous portrait of Ricci that hangs today in the sacristy of the Church of the Gesù in Rome. When Ricci complained of Father Yu's mediocrity as a painter, a second painter was sent to China from Father Niccolo's school in Japan. This painter, Ni Yicheng (alias Jacques Niva or Niwa), S.J. (1579–1638) was born in Japan to a Chinese father and a Japanese mother. He arrived in Macau in 1601 at eighteen years of age and thereafter divided his time between Macau, Nanchang, and Beijing. His religious paintings were in great demand by Chinese Christians. One of his paintings, or a derivative therefrom, was a Chinese version of the Virgin and child after Saint Luke in the Church of Santa Maria Maggiore in Rome.

Many of these Christian pictures presented in China depicted biblical events, particularly those of the Gospels. These biblical events and images of the Virgin Mary had been popular artistic themes among Renaissance and mannerist artists of Europe. These paintings were placed in Christian churches in China and attracted large numbers of interested Chinese. Unfortunately, very few of these early Christian paintings in China have survived. There were also court paintings portraying members of European royal families, such as Louis XIV of France, but these circulated only within the Chinese court.

What circulated to a far wider audience in China than the paintings were the illustrated books and loose sheets of engravings from Europe. These used techniques and pictorial elements that were more adaptable to Chinese ink painting and woodblock printing than the oil paintings of religious themes and European royalty. These illustrated books and engravings featured European landscapes and settings whose realism, perspective, shading, and chiaroscuro are said to have fascinated Chinese artists. Another influential European element was plasticity, the use of tonal contrasts and shadows to give the appearance of three-dimensionality rather than the three-dimensional space used by Chinese artists. Some of these elements had been introduced with Buddhist art a thousand years before but, after arousing some Chinese curiosity and imitation, had faded. Now these techniques from Europe were once again attracting attention in China. European engravings sent to China numbered at least in the hundreds and perhaps in the thousands. The eminent Christian literatus Yang Tingyun (1557–1627) claimed that there were seven thousand European books in China. Although this figure was probably high, a substantial number of these European books were part of the famous Beitang (North Church) Library of Beijing. Many of the books in this collection have been preserved and were catalogued in the 1940s by Father H. Verhaeren.

Some of these European illustrations and engravings were reproduced in Chinese works of art. The most well known of these reproductions were four engravings that appeared in a collection of stone rubbings by Cheng Dayue entitled *The Ink Collection of Mr. Cheng (Cheng shi moyuan)* (1609). These four engravings by noted European engravers featured biblical themes: the destruction of Sodom, engraved by Crispin de Passe; Christ and Saint Peter, by Antonius Wierix after Marin de Vos; the resurrected Christ appearing to his disciples on the road to Emmaus, from Nadal's illustrated history of the Gospel and engraved by one of the Wierix brothers; and the Madonna and child, an engraving made in Father Niccolo's school in Arima, Japan, after a plate by Antonius Wierix, based on the painting of Our Lady of Antigua in Seville. These engravings have been widely reproduced, most recently in Jonathan Spence's *Memory Palace of Matteo Ricci*.

Among the first attempts to intermingle European and Chinese art, the most impressive was a work of illustrations on the life of Jesus produced by Giulio Aleni, S.J. (1582–1649). (See figure 2.3.) Father Aleni's abilities and achievements as a China missionary rank very close to those of Ricci. However, whereas Ricci's work was primarily associated with major cities like Nanjing and Beijing, Aleni worked in the more remote areas of southeast China, particularly in Fujian province. (See map 2.) In his effort to propagate Christianity in Fujian, Aleni used one of the most powerful tools that Europe was then producing: the vivid pictorial images of Renaissance artists, whose sacred images were received with respect and fascination in China.

In the early seventeenth century, the most famous illustrated version of the Gospels was the work *Images of the History of the Gospel (Evangelicae Historiae*

Fig. 2.3. A Chinese engraved portrait of the Jesuit
Father G. Aleni (1582–1649), from his biography,
Taixi Siji Ai xiansheng yulu (post-1649) by Li Sixuan,
cliché Bibliothèque nationale de France. Father Aleni
ranks second only to Father Ricci as the leading Jesuit
of the early modern China mission.

Imagines) (1593) by Gerónimo Nadal, S.J. (1507–1580). Nadal's book combined 153 large engravings with written meditations in a manner influenced by
The Spiritual Exercises of Saint Ignatius Loyola, the founder of the Society of
Jesus. Nadal was so close to Loyola that he is referred to as Loyola's alter ego. In
his famous spiritual manual, *The Spiritual Exercises* (1533), Loyola had developed the technique of using the senses (sight, hearing, smell, and touch) to reinforce Jesus' teachings. We see Nadal using this technique in combining these
vivid illustrations with a written text to convey the life and teachings of Jesus.
The use of these images to convey a faithful representation of Scripture was also
a Catholic response to the Protestant demand for closer adherence to Scripture.

Although the result has sometimes been criticized as being slavish to the printed word, at the time the work was produced, these illustrations were meant not only to narrate the events of Jesus' life but also to serve as a basis for biblical meditations. The use of visual images in mnemonic techniques was still common at that time, although the mnemonic tradition is practically forgotten today.

Because of fears of an examination by the Roman Inquisition, Nadal had not published his work before dying in 1580. The project was taken up by the Jesuit General Claudio Acquaviva. The finest craftsmen in the art of copper engraving in seventeenth-century Europe were found in Antwerp and Amsterdam, and it was in Antwerp that the Jesuits tracked down their favorite engravers in the taverns. The talents of the Wierix brothers Antonius (1555–1603) and Hieronymous (1551–1614) as engravers were surpassed only by their debauchery, drunkenness, and greed for money. After many adjustments to the drawings and protracted negotiations, the Wierix brothers agreed to undertake the task. The production costs were enormous, but the work was finally printed in Antwerp in 1593 and was widely disseminated in Europe.

The publication of Nadal's work was eagerly anticipated by missionaries in East Asia, who as early as 1584 were sending letters to Rome requesting copies. The missionaries realized that holy pictures conveyed the mysteries of the Christian faith in ways that sometimes were more effective than words. In China during the late Ming dynasty there had been a proliferation of printing as an increasingly literate society demanded books in ever greater numbers. In China, unlike in Europe, both books and graphic art were printed with carved wooden blocks. The great demand for printed and graphic materials in China had brought graphic art to its peak of development around 1600. Graphic art was widely employed to inform and to entertain and so it was a popular medium.

By 1605 a copy of Nadal's work had arrived in China. The first Jesuit to attempt to reproduce it in China was made by João da Rocha, S.J. (1565–1623). Father Rocha engaged the well-known scholar and painter Dong Qichang (1555–1636) or one of his students to adapt the illustrations from Nadal's work to China. Later, in 1635–1637 while working in Fuzhou, Aleni and three other Jesuits produced a Chinese version of Nadal's work consisting of fifty engravings and a cover page. It was entitled *The Incarnation of the Lord of Heaven through Illustrations and Commentary.* With considerable effort, the copper engravings of Nadal's work were transformed into Chinese wood carvings, with a delightful result (see figure 2.4).

Gradually the process of sinicizing these European techniques moved forward. Whereas the characters in Cheng Dayue's collection had distinctly European features, the forty-eight pictures on biblical themes presented by Father Schall to the last Ming emperor, the Chongzhen Emperor (r. 1628–1643), in 1640 revealed Chinese features. Three of these pictures were reproduced in the

Fig. 2.4. The Crucifixion of Jesus from Father G. Aleni, *Tianzhu jiang-sheng chuxiang jingjie (Incarnation of the Lord of Heaven through Illustra-tions and Commentary)* (Hangzhou, 1637). Permission of the Archivum Romanum Societatis Iesu, Rome. Father Aleni's work is based upon the famous work *Evangelicae Historiae Imagines* (Antwerp, 1593) by Gerón-imo Nadal, S.J.

notoriously anti-Christian work *I Cannot Do Otherwise* (ca. 1664) by Yang Guangxian described in the next chapter. (See figure 2.5).

耶穌方釘刑架像

第四十二圖

Fig. 2.5. Driving spikes into the body of Jesus as part of the punishment of the Crucifixion. This illustration was originally one of forty-eight drawings on the life of Christ presented by Father Schall to the Chongzheng Emperor in 1640. Yang Guangxian used this illustration in his anti-Christian work *I Cannot Do Otherwise (Budeyi)* (1664) to attack Christianity by showing that Jesus was really an outlaw who was executed for the crimes of rebellion and sedition.

Works Consulted

Chesneaux, Jean. *Peasant Revolts in China, 1840–1949.* Translated by C. A. Curwen. New York: W. W. Norton, 1973.

Cippola, Carlo. *Clocks and Culture, 1300–1700.* New York: W. W. Norton, 1967.

Cohen, Paul A. *China and Christianity: The Missionary Movement and the Growth of Antiforeignism, 1860–1870.* Cambridge: Harvard University Press, 1963.

Dehergne, Joseph. *Répertoire des Jésuites de Chine de 1552 à 1800.* Rome: Institutum Historicum Societatis Iesu, 1973.

Dunne, George H. *Generation of Giants: The Story of the Jesuits in China in the Last Decades of the Ming Dynasty.* Notre Dame, Ind.: University of Notre Dame Press, 1962.

Elvin, Mark. *The Pattern of the Chinese Past: A Social and Economic Interpretation.* Stanford, Calif.: Stanford University Press, 1973.

Foss, Theodore N. "A Western Interpretation of China: Jesuit Cartography." In *East Meets West: The Jesuits in China, 1582–1773*, edited by Charles E. Ronan and Bonnie B. C. Oh, 209–51. Chicago: Loyola University Press, 1988.

Fu, Lo-shu. *A Documentary Chronicle of Sino-Western Relations (1644–1820).* 2 vols. Tucson: University of Arizona Press, 1966.

Hirsch, Bret. *Passions of the Cut Sleeve: The Male Homosexual Tradition in China.* Berkeley and Los Angeles: University of California Press, 1990.

Hudson, G. F. *Europe and China: A Survey of Their Relations from the Earliest Times to 1800.* London: Edward Arnold, 1931.

Hummel, Arthur W., ed. *Eminent Chinese of the Ch'ing Period (1644–1912).* Washington, D.C.: U.S. Government Printing Office, 1943.

Jami, C., and H. Delahaye, eds. *L'Europe en Chine: Interactions scientifiques, religieuses, et culturelles aux dix-septième et dix-huitième siècles.* Paris: De Boccard, 1993.

Kuhn, Philip A. *Soulstealers: The Chinese Sorcery Scare of 1768.* Cambridge: Harvard University Press, 1990.

Mungello, D. E. *The Forgotten Christians of Hangzhou.* Honolulu: University of Hawaii Press, 1994.

———, ed. *The Rites Controversy: Its History and Meaning.* Nettetal, Germany: Steyler, 1994.

Murray, John J. *Antwerp in the Age of Plantin and Brueghel.* Norman: University of Oklahoma Press, 1970.

Peterson, Willard J. "Why Did They Become Christians? Yang T'ing-yün, Li Chih-tsao, and Hsü Kuang-chi." In *East Meets West: The Jesuits in China, 1582–1773,* edited by Charles E. Ronan and Bonnie B. C. Oh, 129–52. Chicago: Loyola University Press, 1988.

Ricci, Matteo. *The True Meaning of the Lord of Heaven (T'ien-chu Shih-i).* Translated by Douglas Lancashire and Peter Hu Kuo-chen. Edited by Edward J. Malatesta.St. Louis: Institute of Jesuit Sources, 1985.

Rocke, Michael. *Forbidden Friendships: Homosexuality and Male Culture in Renaissance Florence.* New York: Oxford University Press, 1996.

Spence, Jonathan D. *The Memory Palace of Matteo Ricci.* New York: Viking, 1984.

Standaert, Nicolas. "New Trends in the Historiography of Christianity in China." *Catholic Historical Review* 83, no. 4 (October 1997): 573–613.

———. *Yang Tingyun: Confucian and Christian in Late Ming China.* Leiden: Brill, 1988.

Ter Haar, B. J. *The White Lotus Teachings in Chinese Religious History.* Leiden: Brill, 1992.

Tsien, Tsuen-hsuin. "Western Impact on China through Translation." *Far Eastern Quarterly* 18 (1954): 305–27.

Väth, Alfons. *Johann Schall von Bell, SJ: Missionar in China, kaiserlicher Astronom, und Ratgeber am Hofe von Peking, 1592–1666.* 1933; rev. ed., Nettetal, Germany: Steyler, 1991.

Verhaeren, H. *Catalogue de la bibliothèque du Pé-t'ang.* Beijing: Lazaristes, 1949.

Wakeman, Frederic, Jr. *The Great Enterprise: The Manchu Reconstruction of Imperial Order in Seventeenth-Century China.* 2 vols. Berkeley and Los Angeles: University of California Press, 1985.

Young, John D. *Confucianism and Christianity: The First Encounter.* Hong Kong: University of Hong Kong Press, 1983.

Zürcher, E. *Bouddhisme, Christianisme, et société chinoise.* Paris: Julliard, 1990.

———. "Confucian and Christian Religiosity in Late Ming China." *Catholic Historical Review* 83, no. 4 (October 1997): 614–53.

Chinese Rejection of Western Culture and Christianity

The Basis of Anti-Christian Feeling in China

Whereas the literati's interest in Christianity weakened (but never died) as the seventeenth century progressed, small numbers of lower-class Chinese continued to be converted by non-Jesuit missionaries, particularly the Franciscans and Dominicans. However, anti-Christian feeling grew in China as the seventeenth and eighteenth centuries progressed.

One basis of anti-Christian feeling in China was Confucian religious skepticism and agnosticism. There is an often quoted passage in the Confucian classic the *Analects* (chap. 11:12) in which Confucius speaks of avoiding spirits. It has never been fully clarified whether Confucius was simply showing respect for spiritual things or whether he was expressing an attitude of agnostic humanism, but where some have seen ambiguity, the Jesuits saw an opportunity for harmonizing Confucianism with Christianity. The Jesuits viewed the lack of religious emphasis in Confucianism as a basis for blending its moral and social strains with the explicitly religious strains of Christianity. Whereas Buddhism and popular Daoism were explicitly religious and fraught with heterodoxies in the eyes of Christians, Confucianism was only implicitly religious and so less explicitly heterodox. Still, there was a strain of religious skepticism in Confucianism that caused many literati to reject the mystical elements of Christianity (the Virgin Birth, the Incarnation, the miraculous healings, the Resurrection, and the Trinity).

A second basis of anti-Christian feeling among the literati was Chinese ethnocentrism, or the belief that Chinese culture was superior to other cultures. The Chinese literati believed in the Transmission of the Way *(Dao tong)* by which truth was passed from the ancients to Confucius and, in turn, to other literati down to the present. Many literati believed that participation in the tradition was necessary for something to be true; they called this tradition "the true Way" *(zheng Dao)*. The false way was referred to by various terms *(xie, yiduan,* and *zuo-dao)*, all of which meant "false" and "heterodox" and carried connotations of being different in a way that was not Chinese.

The Chinese literati were not unique in developing such an ethnocentric view of truth. The Spanish missionaries who came out of a *Reconquista* atmosphere tended to see Christian truth in a similar way. Both the Chinese and Spanish mixed a high degree of cultural factors into their view of religious truth. But just as the Spanish missionaries did not represent the views of all Christian missionaries in China, neither did the ethnocentric views of some literati represent the outlook of all Chinese literati. Literati who converted to Christianity, or who at least were sympathetic to its teachings, believed that the truths of the ancients were not limited to the Chinese, because the ancients spoke primarily as human beings rather than as Chinese. (Europeans who were sympathetic to Chinese philosophy also tended to believe that the biblical patriarchs spoke primarily as human beings rather than as heirs of a Western race.) These literati tended to interpret certain passages from the classics to support their views. For example, Shang Huqing in a preface to *The Touchstone of True Knowledge* (1698) (in Chinese) cited the Confucian classic *Mencius* (chap. IV.b) to make the point that the legendary sage-ruler Shun (2255–2205 B.C.) and King Wen (ca. 1050 B.C.), although originating in places over a thousand *li* (333 miles) apart, with a thousand years separating them, had identical standards as sages. Shang wrote that regardless of whether one's homeland is north, south, east, or west, the minds and principles of the sages are the same. In chapter 2, we noted that the Christian literatus Zhang Xingyao had claimed that "in the Eastern Sea and Western Sea sages arise who are identical in thinking." While Shang and Zhang as Christians constituted a very small percentage of literati, views about the universality of sagehood were widely held among the literati.

From the outset, Christianity evoked hostile sentiments among the Chinese literati who saw it in much the same way that many saw Buddhism and Daoism. These teachings were viewed as false because they were heterodox; in fact, the terms "heterodoxy" and "falsehood" became synonymous. The term "Confucianism" is rarely used by the Chinese and is a Western construct, created by Europeans in the seventeenth century; the Chinese themselves call this philosophy the "Literati Teaching" *(Ruxue)* and it represents a tradition of wisdom handed down from antiquity. Confucius himself said that he was simply transmitting the wisdom of antiquity and not creating it. In fact, to claim the truths associated with the Confucian tradition as a personal creation of Confucius would be to demean them as being the insights of only one man. While it is difficult to trace the truths to their precise ancient forms, it is very clear that the teachings associated with Confucius were further developed in later years by other literati, so that the Confucianism of the seventeenth century (Neo-Confucianism) was far more complex than the philosophy that Confucius himself had taught, although the philosophy certainly attempted to be true to the essential teachings of the master.

The intellectual basis of anti-Christian attitudes in China was found largely in Neo-Confucian thinkers whose opposition to Christianity involved more than ethnocentrism. The intellectual grounds to this opposition derived from Neo-Confucian cosmology, a dimension of Confucian philosophy that had not been developed during Confucius's time. While Confucius himself may have avoided spirits and not discussed transcendent concerns, Neo-Confucian morality was based upon a cosmological ground that had explicit religious dimensions. For this reason, Ricci and other Jesuits criticized Neo-Confucianism and favored the "original Confucianism" of Confucius, which lacked these religious elements that conflicted with Christianity. The most basic element of Neo-Confucian cosmology was *Taiji* (Supreme Ultimate), which generates the world in a way quite different from Christian Creation. (See figure 3.1.) According to Neo-Confucian cosmology formulated in the Song dynasty by Zhou Dunyi (1017–1073) and later incorporated into the Neo-Confucian philosophy of Zhu Xi (1130–1200), the universe consists of ongoing processes of generation and corruption, with different stages occurring simultaneously. The Diagram of the Supreme Ultimate reduces these processes to their simplest level, which begins with unity and then divides into active *yang* and quiescent *yin* forces; yang and yin then further divide into increasing diversity, which eventually returns to unity, and the cycle repeats its course. Neo-Confucians did not see Heaven *(Tian)* as a supreme personal being like the Christians did, and they were highly critical of Ricci's use of the Confucian classics to support Christianity.

Another source of anti-Christian feeling was based on the Chinese fear of subversion. This issue became more important after the Manchus came to power in 1644. The Manchus were military conquerors who constituted a tiny minority in the vast population of China. They lived in a perpetual state of worry over threats to their control of the majority population. This concern caused them to pressure the scholar-officials to be constantly on the alert against subversive activity. The hypersensitivity of the Manchu throne to such activity was demonstrated in the Chinese sorcery scare of 1768, when it was believed that sorcerers were clipping queues (a Manchu-style pigtail shown in figure 1.3 imposed on all Chinese males after the conquest of 1644). Beginning in the lower Yangzi River region near Suzhou, wandering Buddhist monks and other homeless people generated hysteria among the populace by spreading rumors that the sorcerers had the power to use the clipped queue in a form of black magic. The magic was aimed particularly at prized male children, who would become ill, and possibly even die, through the loss of part of their soul. Although the imperial authorities were skeptical of the claims of the sorcerers' powers, they were concerned that

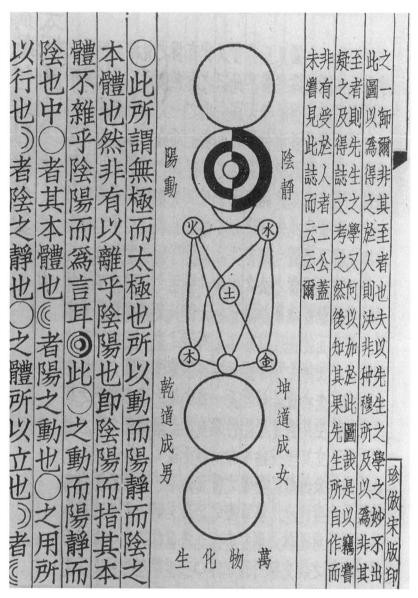

Fig. 3.1. The Diagram of the Supreme Ultimate *(Taiji tu)* by Zhou Dunyi (1017–1073). The Supreme Ultimate was the cornerstone of Neo-Confucian cosmology. This illustration is from the *Xingli jingyi* (Essential meaning of the school of Nature and Principle; i.e., Neo-Confucianism), compiled by Li Guangdi in 1715 by order of the Kangxi Emperor. The diagram represents the different stages of generation and corruption in the universe, with the circles at the top and bottom indicating the cyclical nature of this process. This cyclical nature conflicted with the Judeo-Christian notion of Creation ex nihilo (out of nothing) described in Genesis.

the clipping of queues (an illegal act) signified subversive activity, and Manchu paranoia over this issue exaggerated the danger.

It was the missionaries' foreign status and their association with the aggressive Portuguese and Dutch traders on the southeast coast of China that raised the fear of subversion. Although such a threat might appear ridiculous in light of the relative sizes of China and these European nations in the seventeenth century, the damage done to Chinese shipping and to the coastal villages in Fujian by the European traders was considerable. Moreover, by the end of the eighteenth century, the balance of power had shifted, and beginning in 1839 with the Opium War (or First Anglo-Chinese War), smaller European nations began inflicting a series of humiliating military defeats upon the Chinese. There were isolated European proposals to invade China, but none was implemented. In short, the Manchu fear of subversion from the European missionaries, while greatly exaggerated, was not entirely unfounded.

Another basis for anti-Christian feeling was widespread concern among the Chinese populace that Christian churches might upset the harmony of nature. The Chinese had a very strong belief in geomancy, or *fengshui* (literally, "wind and water"). Geomancy involves the belief that one's fortune can be enhanced by constructing buildings, homes, and graves in harmony with the physical surroundings. Conversely, one could suffer ill fortune if these sites were built in opposition to geomantic forces. The primary geomantic force is called the "cosmic breath" *(qi)*. It consists of the celestial forces of yin and yang, whose outward signs are the physical forms of wind and water. The determination of a building or burial site involves the analysis of factors such as the location, terrain, foundation, surroundings, streams flowing past the site, and the direction or orientation. The aim is to determine the most harmonious placement of the building or grave in relationship to these forces, which, in turn, will produce the most favorable experience for the occupants of the building and the descendants of the deceased in the grave. The construction of Christian, particularly European-style, churches, and especially towers and crosses on the exterior was sometimes believed to violate the harmony of the geomantic forces in the area and was thought to create an unfavorable atmosphere for those Chinese who lived and worked nearby.

Yet another basis of anti-Christian feeling directed toward the European priests was a fear that they would seduce Chinese women. This was particularly the case among upper-class families where the women were largely secluded within the home. In seventeenth- and eighteenth-century China, Christian churches were often built with separate chapels for women. However, certain rites required close contact between the priest and women. In the administration of the sacraments, which involved touching the women, priests were sometimes accused of fondling their breasts. Accusations of improprieties in the act of confession were sometimes handled by having a mat hung between the priest and confessant with an observer at the other end of the room, close enough to see that nothing improper happened between the priest and the woman confessing, yet far enough away so that the words of the confession and the priest's response could not be heard.

These restrictions did not prevent women from taking an active part in the Chinese church. One notable example was Candida Xu (1607–1680), the granddaughter of one of the Three Pillars, Xu Guangqi (see figure 3.2). In many Chinese families, the baptism of a prominent family member would lead to the conversion of the entire family. This was the case with the baptism of Madame Xu, who, after the death of her husband in 1653, became a benefactress of the church. She financed the construction of 135 chapels in the area of Shanghai, paid for the publication of religious and devotional books, and generously supported the missionary church work and the poor. She became known to Europeans when the missionary Philippe Couplet, S.J., wrote a book on her life that was published in French in Paris in 1688.

A final basis of anti-Christian feeling was the belief that the missionaries practiced some form of alchemy. Daoist alchemy in China involved two very different goals, although in both cases chemical laboratories were used. One was an attempt to transmute base metals into silver and the other was an attempt to synthesize an elixir of immortality. The substance most commonly associated with this elixir was mercury in the form of its primary ore, cinnabar (red mercuric sulfide). When Ricci taught Christian immortality in China, many people confused Christian immortality with Daoist immortality, especially when Portuguese traders bought large quantities of mercury in Canton. The boats on which this mercury was shipped to Japan and India returned carrying silver, reinforcing the belief that the Europeans and missionaries were practicing alchemy. Ricci found these suspicions frustrating, particularly since Daoist immortality was physical and aimed at prolonging the life of the body whereas Christian immortality was spiritual and focused on the soul. He was constantly dealing with Chinese who were attracted to him for the wrong reason, namely, his supposed alchemical expertise rather than his spiritual teaching.

Chinese Anti-Christian Movements

While anti-Christian sentiments among the literati were constantly present, only occasionally did they break out into anti-Christian movements; this occurred periodically throughout the seventeenth century. The first anti-Christian movement was centered in Nanjing in the years 1616–1621. It was instigated by the scholar-official Shen Que, who sought to uncover a subversive movement out of

Madame Candide Hiu petite fille du Grand Chancellier de la Chine, Illustre pour sa piete Elle mourut le 24 octobre 1680, agée de 73 ans dans la Province de Nankim.

Paris chez Nolin

Fig. 3.2. Madame Candida Xu (1607–1680), an early Christian convert and benefactress of Christianity, from Philippe Couplet, S.J., *History of a Christian Lady of China (Histoire d'une dame chrétienne de la Chine)* (Paris, 1688). Permission of Harold B. Lee Library, Brigham Young University.

animosity toward Christians and to advance his own political career. In his petitions to the throne, Shen accused the foreign priests of misleading the people into following a criminal (Jesus) who was sentenced to death. He accused the missionaries of teaching the people to neglect their ancestors, offering money for conversions, and practicing rites that involved mixed sexes in debauchery. Shen accused the missionaries of cultivating high officials and gaining access to official documents. He claimed that they maintained contacts with the Portuguese at Macau who were dangerous foreigners. He voiced suspicion about the missionaries' mysterious sources of funding.

Shen accused the missionaries of holding weekly secret meetings, controlling the people through magic arts, and keeping records of the names of their fellow conspirators. Shen noted similarities between these Christians and the outlawed White Lotus sect. (Christian converts on a higher social level were accused by Shen of constituting a literati faction.) The priests at Nanjing were arrested, and their residence was searched and an inventory made of the contents, but no weapons were found. Four Jesuits were expelled to Macau but the expulsion was of short duration. The persecution was largely limited to Nanjing and no one was put to death because of it. In the aftermath of the Nanjing persecution, the first collection of anti-Christian literature, *A Collection of Works Attacking Heterodoxy (Poxieji)*, appeared in 1639.

Far more destructive was the anti-Christian movement led from Beijing by the scholar-official Yang Guangxian beginning in 1664. Like Shen, Yang had an intense dislike of Christians, though his motives appear to have been more sincere and less for personal advancement. In fact, Yang appears to have been a dedicated Neo-Confucian who genuinely believed that Christianity was intellectually false and harmful to China. However, the intensity of Yang's beliefs led him to conduct a harsh attack against Father Schall that caused the execution of several of Schall's assistants. Yang accused Schall of causing the death of the Xiaoxian Empress, and—because of the Shunzhi Emperor's grief over the loss of his favorite concubine—the premature death of the Shunzhi Emperor himself. The basis of the accusation was that as head of the Bureau of Astronomy, Schall had brought this death about by selecting an inauspicious day for the burial of an imperial prince born to the Xiaoxian Empress and the Shunzhi Emperor. In the intense political atmosphere of the court, this charge gained credibility among the shamanistically-minded Manchus and an investigation was begun.

In the course of the investigation in early 1665, Schall, who was nearly seventy-three years old, suffered a stroke and became paralyzed. He had to be carried into the legal proceedings on a stretcher and had lost the ability to speak. He was assisted by Father Verbiest. Schall was found guilty and, along with the seven Chinese astronomers who assisted him, was sentenced to a lingering death. Later five more Chinese were sentenced to death and the three Jesuits besides Schall then in Beijing were sentenced to flogging and exile. The day after the judgment, an earthquake struck Beijing and a fire occurred in the palace. These were interpreted as acts of God that indicated Heaven's displeasure over the verdicts. All of the accused were freed except for five Chinese Christian astronomers, who served as scapegoats. They were blamed for choosing the inauspicious day of the prince's burial and were executed. The four Jesuits in Beijing were allowed to remain there, but all other missionaries were expelled to Macau until 1671 and the Christian churches in China were closed.

Yang was appointed in Schall's place to head the Bureau of Astronomy but he was incompetent and unable to produce an accurate calendar. Father Verbiest challenged Yang and his associates to a competition involving an astronomical computation. When Western methods proved more accurate in several trials, Yang was removed as head of the bureau and replaced by Verbiest. Schall died on 15 August 1666, and soon thereafter the Kangxi Emperor ordered a review of the case. The verdicts against Schall and the executed Chinese astronomers were posthumously reversed, while Yang was disgraced and sentenced to death. In light of Yang's advanced age, his sentence was commuted to exile and he was allowed to return to his native home. Sick and weary, he died during the journey; but even from the grave Yang's spirit did not give up: a rumor circulated that the missionaries had poisoned him.

Yang wrote a caustically anti-Christian polemic entitled *I Cannot Do Otherwise (Budeyi)* in which he included illustrations of the Crucifixion (see figure 2.5). Yang argued that these pictures confirmed that Jesus was a subversive rebel leader (not unlike subversive rebels in China) who was convicted and executed for his crimes. For the Confucian literati, who were the guardians of law and order in China, such criticism was especially damning and it found strong support among the literati. Although the Kangxi Emperor issued an edict of toleration of Christianity in 1692, his son, the Yongzheng Emperor, issued a countervailing edict in 1724 declaring Christianity a heterodox sect and closing the churches. Most of the missionaries were expelled, first to Canton and then to Macau, from 1724 to 1736. During this time, an underground church emerged in China with a number of missionaries secretly visiting their flocks, instructing neophytes, and baptizing converts. Christianity continued to suffer from severe restrictions under the long reign of the Qianlong Emperor (r. 1736–1796).

In recent years, two Sinologists have offered influential explanations for the rejection of Christianity in China. The French Sinologist Jacques Gernet in a widely read book translated into English argued that Christianity was unable to be assimilated in China because of fundamental cultural differences between China and Europe. According to Gernet, irreconcilable differences in the ways Chinese and Europeans thought were produced by linguistic differences in the Chinese and Indo-European languages. He argues that Greek philosophy and medieval Scholastic philosophy could not have developed had they been based upon the Chinese language because the latter lacks the verb "to be" and the concept of "being." He argues that there was no Chinese word to denote the concept of being or essence. The Chinese were not philosophically unsophisticated, and Gernet claims that they were the only civilization not based on the Indo-European languages to develop complete philosophical thought. Whereas the Indo-European languages were well suited to fostering the Christian elements of transcendental and immutable realities, the Chinese language was more inclined to see realities in terms of the senses, which are transitory. Gernet's interpretation has been much disputed, but one should note that he uses it to explain that the Chinese reaction to Christianity was not merely xenophobic but rather was based upon cultural differences.

The Dutch Sinologist Erik Zürcher offers a different explanation for the failure of Christianity to be assimilated into seventeenth- and eighteenth-century China. Drawing from his earlier study of the assimilation of Buddhism into China early in the first millennium, Zürcher argues that Christianity was rejected because of the overly centralized manner in which the Jesuits were directed by a Counter-Reformation church and because of the incompatibility in China of the Jesuit dual roles of scholar and priest.

Both of these explanations contain valid elements but they are incomplete. The Chinese rejection of Christianity was neither total nor permanent. Christianity continued to ebb and flow in its development in China, although sometimes it has given the appearance of being exterminated. As recently as the early 1970s, it was believed by many China scholars that Christianity had been largely eradicated in China, but later events proved that the religion had merely been driven underground by persecution. It could be argued that seeds sown by Christian missionaries in the sixteenth through the eighteenth centuries simply took several centuries to harvest. Such a long-term perspective is particularly appropriate for a nation with a history as long as China's.

European Art at the Chinese Court

The encounter between European and Chinese visual arts occurred in two different areas: at the imperial court and outside of the court in the churches and among the literati. Whereas the demands of the court produced mere imitation of Western style by Chinese craftsmen-artists, the encounter among the literati stimulated some creative responses among literati-artists. However, the Western influence upon Chinese artists was not widespread and was limited to a small number of literati-artists.

Although Ricci had established the first Jesuit residence in Beijing in 1601, it was not until after the Manchu conquest in 1644 that European painters worked at the imperial court. The first of these mostly Jesuit European painters appears to have been Johann Grueber, S.J. (1623–1680), of Austria. Perhaps the greatest Manchu ruler was the Kangxi Emperor (r. 1662–1722) and the first European painter at his court was the Jesuit lay brother Cristoforo Fiori, a twenty-four-year-old Italian who arrived at the court in 1694. Nothing is known of his artistic work and, finding religious life too demanding, Fiori left the Jesuit order in 1705.

Perspective was an artistic technique that attracted Chinese to Christian churches. The layman Giovanni Gherardini of Bologna was brought to Beijing by Father Joachim Bouvet in 1700, probably because of the frescoes he had produced in the Jesuit headquarters at Paris, which excelled in perspective. In Beijing Gherardini decorated the walls, ceiling, and cupola of the new European-style Jesuit Church of Our Savior with frescoes of striking perspective, which intrigued Chinese visitors. In addition, he taught perspective and oil painting to Chinese students. But Gherardini was unhappy with the strictures of religious life in Beijing and stayed for only four years before returning to France in 1704. Nevertheless, the effects of his visit remained and Father Ripa reported seeing seven or eight of Gherardini's students in 1715 painting Chinese landscapes in oils on sturdy Korean paper. Fathers Verbiest and Ludovici Buglio, S.J. (1606–1682) of Sicily were not artists but contributed by teaching perspective to Chinese students. The literati and the Kangxi Emperor were so fascinated by the artistic technique of drawing perspective that the Jesuits produced a Chinese adaptation of the famous work on perspective by Andrea Pozzo, S.J. (1642–1709), *Perspectiva pictorum et architectorum* (1698). The Jesuit lay brother Giuseppe Castiglione (1688–1766) of Milan collaborated with the high official Nien Xiyao to produce a work intended primarily for Chinese painters, *Visual Learning (Shixue),* in two editions, 1729 and 1735.

Father Bouvet also brought the Jesuit lay brother Charles de Belleville (1657–1730) from France to Beijing in 1700. Belleville was an artist of diverse talents, including sculpture, painting of miniature portraits, and architecture. He completed the Church of Our Savior in 1703 and taught painting to young eunuchs at the court. However, unable to tolerate the harsh climate of Beijing, he returned to Europe in 1707.

The next artist to arrive was Matteo Ripa (1682–1746) of Naples. Ripa was not associated with the Jesuits. He had been trained and sent out by the Sacred Congregation for the Propagation of the Faith (Propaganda Fide) and was affiliated with the ill-fated embassy of the papal legate Thomas Maillard de Tournon, who was an opponent of the Jesuits. Nevertheless, the Kangxi Emperor valued artistic talent so highly that he did not allow his negative feelings toward Cardinal Tournon to deny him the services of a capable artist. Consequently, in 1712 the emperor asked Father Ripa to draw thirty-six views of his summer mountain retreat near Rehe (Jehol) in Manchuria and then etch them on copper. Ripa tried to decline the assignment on the grounds that he was a portrait painter rather than a landscape artist and moreover he had no experience in making copper engravings. However, the emperor insisted and Ripa completed the assignment in 1714, producing the first copper engravings in China, where wood engravings had traditionally been used. That same year the Kangxi Emperor ordered Ripa to make copper engravings of the Jesuit map of China, Manchuria, and Korea. This was done in forty-four plates.

Ripa appears to have been a restless man, driven by powerful motivations. He and the two other Propaganda missionaries who arrived at the Beijing court in February 1711 were the first non-Jesuit missionaries to serve there. However, during his thirteen years at the court, Ripa developed an enormous dislike for the Jesuits. After becoming disillusioned by events at the Chinese court and by Jesuit dominance there, he turned his interest in another direction, that of developing a native Chinese clergy. To this end, he gathered a number of Chinese boys whom he began to train. He spent so much time with these boys, who accompanied him everywhere in his carriage, that criticism and sexual innuendoes began to be circulated by Jesuits as well as Chinese officials. After the death of the Kangxi Emperor in December 1722, Ripa decided to return with the boys to Naples.

Ripa departed from Beijing in November of 1723 with his entourage of four boys and a Chinese teacher. At Canton they took passage on an English ship and were harassed by the crew. They survived the crew's hostility and the bad weather to arrive in London, where King George I invited all six of them to dine at the palace. Ripa presented a copy of his map of China, Japan, and Manchuria to King George and it is preserved in the British Museum to this day. Arriving back in Naples, Ripa overcame many frustrations, including financial problems and the animosity of fellow clerics, to found a Chinese College (Collegio dei Cinesi) in 1732. The Chinese College in Naples lasted until 1888, training 108 Chinese priests. In 1743 at sixty-one years of age, Ripa began composing a journal, which was published in 1832 in Italian and appeared in a condensed English translation at London in 1844.

The most famous Jesuit artist in China was Castiglione. Because of the difficulty in retaining artists in Beijing, the Jesuits sought to find a dedicated member of their order who was also a skilled artist. This individual was found in the lay brother Castiglione, a prolific artist whose canvases painted in churches in Genoa and Coimbra (Portugal) are still extant. He arrived in Beijing in December 1715. Almost immediately the Kangxi Emperor tried to induce him and Father Ripa to paint in enamels but they both resisted until released from the assignment. (Later, in 1719, a trained enameler arrived in Beijing in the person of the Jesuit lay brother Jean-Baptist Gravereau, who unfortunately was forced to return to France in 1722 because of illness.)

Castiglione served three emperors (the Kangxi, Yongzheng, and Qianlong Emperors) for fifty-one years until his death in 1766. In addition to producing numerous paintings, he helped to design the Summer Palace (Yuanmingyuan) in the western suburbs of Beijing. Although Castiglione came trained in oils, the dominant medium of European painters since the sixteenth century, oil painting was not an object of great enthusiasm among the Chinese. On one notable occasion, the Qianlong Emperor complained about the hasty darkening of some poorly mixed oil paints. Nevertheless, the court utilized the missionary artists' realistic skills in portrait painting. Members of the royal family and court officials enthusiastically sat for portraits, and the Qianlong Emperor himself sat for three painters (Castiglione, Ignaz Sichelbarth, S.J. [1708–1780], of Bohemia, and Giuseppi Panzi, S.J. [1734–1812], of Florence).

From both an artistic and a missionary point of view, Jesuit painters at the palace in Beijing faced many restrictions. They were forced to serve long hours in the imperial workshop, working alongside Chinese court painters and craftsmen who had a low status in the palace. The atmosphere was competitive and sometimes hostile. Both the content and style of their artistic work were determined by imperial commands. Jean-Denis Attiret, S.J. (1702–1768), who had come to decorate Jesuit churches, ended up painting endless portraits of members of the imperial family. Nevertheless, the missionary artists Castiglione, Sichelbarth, and Attiret were honored with high official rank by the Qianlong Emperor. Oftentimes they worked in collaboration with Chinese artists, as in portraits in which the European artists painted the faces while the Chinese artists did the costumes and backgrounds. This produced an eclectic Sino-European style in which Western influence in court painting reached its peak. The genres of imperial portraits and, to a lesser extent, landscape and architecture demonstrate this influence by which the use of perspective, chiaroscuro, and realism all appear. Sino-European style began under the Kangxi Emperor with the court painters Jiao Bingzhen and his pupil Leng Mei and peaked under the Qianlong Emperor, after which it went into decline.

Chinese artists known to have studied European painting and perspective under these missionaries included Ding Guanpeng, Zou Yigui, Shen Quan, and Xu Yang, in addition to the previously mentioned Yu Wenhui (Manuel Pereira), Ni Yucheng (Jacques Niva), Jiao Bingzhen, and Leng Mei. Ironically, the well-known painter and poet Wu Li (Wu Yushan) (1632–1718) was ordained as a Jesuit priest but exhibited no apparent Western influence in his paintings.

European Art among the Chinese Literati-Painters

Because of the lack of literary documentation, it is difficult (and even controversial) to identify the Chinese professional and literati gentlemen painters who were influenced by European art. Nevertheless, by comparing their artworks to European works of art then circulating in China, several such artists have been identified. Most of them lived in the region of the lower Yangzi River and had access to Nanjing, an active missionary center believed to be the primary channel through which European artistic influence was spread to these Chinese artists.

The portraits of Zeng Jing (1568–1650) demonstrate a clear Western influence. Zeng was a native of the coastal province of Fujian, where there was considerable contact with missionaries and Portuguese traders. Later he moved to
Nanjing, where Ricci was active around 1600 and where Zeng could have been
exposed to European paintings and prints. Zeng incorporated Western realism
into his portraits by applying many layers of color washes to a light ink outline.
The effect produced features on the faces of his portraits that were akin to
chiaroscuro. Using this technique, Zeng was able to paint portraits that reflect
individualized qualities of personality and character. The creative power of
Zeng's portraits was such that he had many followers among the Bochen School
of professional portrait painters. Much debate has surrounded the claim that the
famous Ming scholar-official painter Dong Qichang (1555–1636) produced an
album of six paintings under the influence of an engraving by Antonius Wierix.
These paintings, found today in the Museum of Natural History in New York,
are signed with Dong's brush name, Xuan Cai, but the name may have been
added by an art dealer.

The influence of European art upon Chinese painting has until recent times
been regarded as minimal. Chinese landscape painting has been held in very high
regard as a unique art form that differed from European painting both in technical medium (ink rather than oil) and content (stylized and abstract images of
nature rather than realistic images and individualized portraits). In addition, the
lack of documentation of contacts between Chinese artists and European art has
been taken as confirmation of an absence of influence.

The art historian Michael Sullivan has argued that there were two main rea-
sons for the lack of influence of European art on Chinese art. First, the number
of Chinese artists who came into contact with European art was very small and
consequently the band of contact was very narrow. The two main points of contact were among the Nanjing School of painters in the seventeenth century and
at the court in Beijing throughout the eighteenth century. As the eighteenth century progressed, the Manchu throne grew increasingly defensive in mentality and
reduced its contacts with Chinese literati and literati-painters, further reducing
the contacts between the European artists at court and the Chinese literati. By
1775 the former missionaries reported that the Qianlong Emperor had lost
interest in his earlier plan of having European artists teach their skills to Chinese
painters.

The second reason for the lack of Western influence on Chinese artists is that
in traditional China, it was the literati and not the court who established artistic
standards. Most Chinese literati who had come into contact with Western art
believed that its techniques of perspective and chiaroscuro were impressive, but
in the manner of artisans (craftsmen) rather than artists. Although Western
painting would be more appreciated by the emerging merchant classes in the

Fig. 3.3. Cityscape, an anonymous engraving from *Civitates Orbis Terrarum* by Georg Braun and Franz Hogenberg, vol. 4 (Cologne, 1572–1616). Herzog August Bibliothek Wolfenbüttel: 7.4 Hist. 2°. By 1600 this volume had been carried to China, where it circulated among Chinese who were in contact with the missionaries. The suspension of the objects in the engraving between diagonally opposite corners is said to have influenced the Chinese painting *Scene from the Jiao Garden,* shown in figure 3.4.

coastal areas of China during the late eighteenth and early nineteenth centuries, the literati remained the cultural arbiters of Chinese artistic taste until the late nineteenth century.

James Cahill has argued, contrary to the view of most art historians, that paintings by certain Chinese artists of the seventeenth and eighteenth centuries do reveal a European influence. Although the eighteenth-century influence, known through the paintings of Castiglione, is more well known, its effect upon Chinese painters was slight. Cahill believes that the seventeenth-century influence was far more creative and important in the history of Chinese painting. To support this view, Cahill compares some late Ming paintings with late-sixteenth-century German engravings of towns and cities (see figures 3.3 and 3.4). The European engravings are drawn from a famous six-volume work published in Cologne in the years 1572–1616 entitled *Civitatis Orbis Terrarum* by Georg

Fig. 3.4. *Scene from the Jiao Garden*. Leaf from an album dated 1625 by Shen Shichong (active ca. 1611–1640). Permission of the National Palace Museum, Taipei, Taiwan, Republic of China. According to the art historian James Cahill, the suspension of the objects in the picture between diagonally opposite corners was an artistic convention influenced by the Chinese artist's exposure to European cityscapes, and quite possibly the cityscape from *Civitates Orbis Terrarum* shown in figure 3.3.

Braun and Franz Hogenberg. The first volume was circulating in China by 1608 and the other volumes followed shortly thereafter.

One of the unique features of the picture-maps (cityscapes) was the oblique angle of view. Braun felt that the viewer of his drawing of a town should be able to look into all the roads, streets, buildings, and open spaces. Consequently, the ground plane of his cityscapes was tilted upward from the back and sideways, so that the elements of the picture were drawn diagonally from one lower corner to the other upper corner. An example of this is presented in the cityscape from *Civitatis Orbis Terrarum* in figure 3.3.

The perspective of Braun and Hogenberg differed greatly from that of traditional Chinese landscape paintings, which for centuries had looked at the scenery straight on. Nevertheless, Cahill has discovered Chinese paintings of the early seventeenth century, when the Braun and Hogenberg volumes were circulating in China, that duplicate this oblique perspective. The scene from the Jiao Garden (figure 3.4) painted by Shen Shichong in 1625 duplicates the perspective shown in figure 3.3 by suspending objects in the picture between diagonally opposite corners. The striking parallels found in these comparisons are caused, according to Cahill, not by the Chinese artist consciously imitating the European pictures, but rather by some more indirect influence after the exposure of these northern European pictures to the visual memories of Chinese artists.

If the Chinese artists had copied or imitated the European pictures, the influence would be clearer but more superficial. Rather, Cahill argues, the Chinese artists' exposure to European pictures was a powerful stimulus to their creativity; he believes the signs of that influence are found in the most original paintings in China at that time. In such powerfully creative artists, conscious imitation of European pictures was unlikely, but once an artist saw the European works and absorbed them into his visual memory, then he (consciously or unconsciously) was influenced by the European models. The result was that European art was used creatively by a small number of Chinese artists to expand the traditional limits of their imaginative experience.

Painters whom Cahill and Sullivan identify as influenced by European techniques include Zhang Hong (1577–after 1652) of Suzhou; Wu Bin (active ca. 1568–1625) of Fujian province and later Nanjing; Shen Shichong (active ca. 1611–1640) of Songjiang; Shao Mi (active 1620–1660) of Suzhou; Zhao Zuo (active ca. 1610–1630), who was a close friend of leading artist Dong Qichang (1555–1636); Cui Zizhong (active 1600–1644); Gong Xian (ca. 1640–1689); the greatest of Nanjing painters, Li Yin (active ca. 1700) of Yangzhou; and Xiang Shengmo (1597–1658). Apart from landscapes, Sullivan claims that direct borrowing from Western sources is seen in the study of flowers and butterflies by Chen Hongshou (1598–1652). In summary, we can say that the influence of European art upon Chinese artists was limited but significant.

Most early Christian churches in China were built in the Chinese style, but because the Jesuit missionaries wished to distinguish their churches from Buddhist temples, a few churches were built in the baroque style, modeled after that most famous of baroque churches, Il Gesù in Rome. The cornerstone of St. Paul's (originally Mother of God) Church in Macau was laid in 1602. Although a fire in 1835 destroyed most of the church, the façade with statuary has survived as a commanding structure at the top of a broad stairway of 130 steps (see figure 3.5). To date, both the architect and its exact European model are uncertain.

In Beijing, shortly before Ricci died in 1610, he initiated the construction of a church modeled after Rome's Il Gesù and St. Paul's in Macau. The church was to be built in European style as an architectural witness to Christianity. Ricci collected fifty silver taels from the Christian scholar-official Li Zhizao and another donor. After Ricci's death, the church was constructed by Father Sabatino de Ursis, S.J. It was built in the central part of Beijing near the Xuanwu Gate on land where the Jesuit residence was located. The church is described by an eyewitness account of 1635 as narrow and long (approximately forty-five feet by twenty-four feet) with a canopy-like ceiling, elaborate windows, and fine paintings done in

Fig. 3.5. The façade of the Church of St. Paul in Macau, whose cornerstone was laid in 1602. Courtesy of the Macau Government Tourist Office. The church was designed by European Jesuits and built with the assistance of Japanese Christian craftsmen who had fled religious persecution in Nagasaki. The church burned in 1835, leaving only the façade and the staircase.

Western style. Over the altar stood a painting of Jesus, whose lifelike appearance Chinese painting is said to have been unable to match. To the right of the hall was a chapel (probably for women) of the Virgin Mary, who was painted as a young girl holding the child Jesus. One of the most beautiful churches in China was a baroque-style church built in 1659–1663 in Hangzhou at the initiative of Father

Martino Martini. This church was very clearly modeled on Il Gesù in Rome and has survived to the present day, though the many devotional paintings that originally filled the church were destroyed by fire in 1692.

In conclusion, although there was a broad-based rejection of Western culture and Christianity in seventeenth- and eighteenth-century China, the rejection was not total. Elements from Western religion and painting entered Chinese culture, and some of these elements would serve as seeds that, in the case of Christianity, would take many years to bear fruit.

Works Consulted

Barnard, Henri. "L'art chrétien en Chine du temps du P. Matthieu Ricci." *Revue d'histoire des missions* (Paris) 12 (1935): 199–229.

Brooks, E. Bruce, and A. Taeko Brooks. *The Original Analects: Sayings of Confucius and His Successors*. New York: Columbia University Press, 1998.

Cahill, James. *The Compelling Image: Nature and Style in Seventeenth-Century Chinese Painting*. Cambridge: Harvard University Press, 1982.

———. "Wu Pin and His Landscape Paintings." In *Proceedings of the International Symposium on Chinese Painting*, 637–98 plus 34 plates. Taipei: National Palace Museum, 1972.

Cameron, Nigel. *Barbarians and Mandarins: Thirteen Centuries of Western Travellers in China*. London: John Weatherhill, 1970.

Chan, Wing-tsit. "The *Hsing-li ching-i* and the Ch'eng-Chu School of the Seventeenth Century." In *The Unfolding of Neo-Confucianism*, edited by William Theodore de Bary, 543–79. New York: Columbia University Press, 1975.

Chaves, Jonathan. *Singing of the Source: Nature and God in the Poetry of the Chinese Painter Wu Li*. Honolulu: University of Hawaii Press, 1993.

Ch'en, Yüan. "Wu Yü-shan. In Commemoration of the 250th Anniversary of His Ordination to the Priesthood in the Society of Jesus." Adapted to English by Eugene Feifel. *Monumenta Serica* 3 (1937–38): 130–70b.

Cohen, Paul A. *China and Christianity*. Cambridge: Harvard University Press, 1963.

De Groot, J. J. M. *Religious System of China*. Leiden: Brill, 1897. 3: 935–1056.

Dehergne, Joseph. *Répertoire des Jésuites de Chine de 1552 à 1800*. Rome: Institutum Historicum Societatis Iesu, 1973.

Dudink, Adrian. "The Inventories of the Jesuit House at Nanking Made Up during the Persecution of 1616–1617 (Shen Que, *Nangong shudu*, 1620)." In *Western Humanistic Culture Presented to China by Jesuit Missionaries (Seventeenth and Eighteenth Centuries)*, edited by Federico Masini, 119–57. Rome: Institutum Historicum Societatis Iesu, 1996.

Eitel, Ernest J. *Feng-shui*. Singapore: Graham Brash, 1985. First published in the *Chinese Recorder and Missionary Journal*, March 1872.

Fong, Wen. Review of James Cahill's *The Compelling Image*. In *Art Bulletin* 68, no. 3 (September 1986): 504–8.

Fu, Lo-shu. *Documentary Chronicle of Sino-Western Relations (1644–1820).* Tucson: University of Arizona Press, 1966.

Gernet, Jacques. *China and the Christian Impact: A Conflict of Cultures.* Translated by Janet Lloyd. Cambridge: Cambridge University Press, 1985.

Hsiang, Ta. "European Influences on Chinese Art in the Later Ming and Early Ch'ing Period." Translated by Wang Teh-chao. *Renditions* 6 (1976): 152–78.

Hwang, Jane. "The Early Jesuits' Printings in China in the Bavarian State Library and the University Library of Munich." In *Collected Essays of the International Symposium on Chinese-Western Cultural Interchange in Commemoration of the Four-Hundredth Anniversary of the Arrival of Matteo Ricci, S.J. in China,* edited by Kuang Lo, 281–93. Taipei: Fu Jen, 1983.

Jennes, Jos. "L'art chrétien en Chine au début du dix-septième siècle (une gravure d'Antoine Wierx identifiée comme modèle d'une peinture de Tong K'i-tch'ang)." *T'oung Pao* 33 (1937): 129–33.

Kao, Mayching. "European Influences in Chinese Art, Sixteenth to Eighteenth Centuries." In *China and Europe: Images and Influences in Sixteenth to Eighteenth Centuries,* edited by Thomas H. C. Lee, 251–81. Hong Kong: Chinese University Press, 1991.

King, Gail. "Couplet's Biography of Madame Candida Xu (1607–1680)." *Sino-Western Cultural Relations Journal* 18 (1996): 41–56.

———. "Note on a Late Ming Dynasty Chinese Description of 'Ricci's Church' in Beijing." *Sino-Western Cultural Relations Journal* 20 (1998): 49–51.

Kuhn, Philip A. *Soulstealers: The Chinese Sorcery Scare of 1768.* Cambridge: Harvard University Press, 1990.

Laufer, Berthold. "Christian Art in China." *Mitteilungen des Seminars für Orientalistische Sprachen* (1910): 100–118 plus plates.

Loehr, George. "Missionary-Artists at the Manchu Court." *Transactions of the Oriental Ceramic Society* (London) 34 (1962–63): 51–67.

McCall, John E. "Early Jesuit Art in the Far East. Part 4: In China and Macao before 1635." *Artibus Asiae* 11 (1949): 45–69.

Mungello, D. E. *Forgotten Christians of Hangzhou.* Honolulu: University of Hawaii Press, 1994.

———, ed. *The Rites Controversy: Its History and Meaning.* Nettetal, Germany: Steyler, 1994.

Needham, Joseph. *Science and Civilisation in China.* 7 vols. in progress. Cambridge: Cambridge University Press, 1954– . See esp. vols. 2 and 3.

Pelliot, Paul. "Les 'Conquêtes de l'empereur de la Chine.'" *T'oung Pao* 20 (1921): 183–274.

———. "La peinture et la gravure européennes en Chine au temps de Mathieu Ricci." *T'oung Pao* 20 (1920–21): 1–18.

———. "Les influences euopéennes sur l'art chinois au dix-septième et au dix-huitième siècle." Conférence faite au Musée Guimet le 20 février 1927. Paris: Imprimerie National, 1948.

Rheinbay, Paul. "Nadal's Religious Iconography Reinterpreted by Aleni for China." In *Scholar from the West: Giulio Aleni S.J. (1582–1649) and the Dialogue between Christianity and China,* edited by Tiziana Lippiello and Roman Malek, 323–34. Nettetal, Germany: Steyler, 1997.

Spence, Jonathan D. *The Memory Palace of Matteo Ricci.* New York: Viking, 1984.

Sullivan, Michael. "The Chinese Response to Western Art." *Art International* 24 (3–4) (November–December 1980): 8–31.

———. *The Meeting of Eastern and Western Art from the Sixteenth Century to the Present Day.* New York: New York Graphic Society, 1973.

———. "Some Possible Sources of European Influence on Late Ming and Early Ch'ing Painting." In *Proceedings of the International Symposium on Chinese Painting,* 595–625 plus 9 plates. Taipei: Fu Jen, 1972.

Swiderski, Richard M. "The Dragon and the Straightedge: A Semiotics of the Chinese Response to European Pictorial Space." *Semiotica* 81 (1–2) (1990): 1–41; 82 (1–2) (1990): 43–136; and 82 (3–4) (1990): 211–68.

Taixeira, Manuel. "The Church of St. Paul in Macau." *Studia* (Lisbon) 41–42 (1979): 51–111 plus 3 illustrations.

Vanderstappen, Harrie. "Chinese Art and the Jesuits in Peking." In *East Meets West: The Jesuits in China, 1582–1773,* edited by Charles E. Ronan and Bonnie B. C. Oh, 103–26. Chicago: Loyola University Press, 1988.

Verhaeren, H. *Catalogue de la bibliothèque du Pé-tang.* Beijing: Lazaristes, 1949.

Voet, Leon. *The Golden Compasses: A History and Evaluation of the Printing and Publishing Activities of the Officina Plantiniana at Antwerp.* 2 vols. Amsterdam: Vangendt, 1972.

Waley, Arthur. "Ricci and Tung ch'i-ch'ang." *T'oung Pao* 2 (1922): 342–43.

Young, John D. *Confucianism and Christianity: The First Encounter.* Hong Kong: University of Hong Kong Press, 1983.

Zürcher, E. *Bouddhisme, Christianisme, et société chinoise.* Paris: Julliard, 1990.

———. "The First Anti-Christian Movement in China (Nanking, 1616–1621)." In *Acta Orientalia Neerlandica,* edited by P. W. Pestman, 188–95. Leiden: Brill, 1971.

———. "Giulio Aleni's Chinese Biography." In *Scholar from the West: Giulio Aleni S.J. (1582–1649) and the Dialogue between Christianity and China,* edited by Tiziana Lippiello and Roman Malek, 85–127. Nettetal, Germany: Steyler, 1997.

4

European Acceptance of Chinese Culture and Confucianism

Jesuit Accommodation and the Chinese Rites Controversy

Why did Europeans admire Chinese culture and why did they want to borrow the philosophy of Confucius? Europeans were influenced by China because they regarded Chinese culture as superior and they were receptive to borrowing from China, at least until the end of the eighteenth century.

The positive reaction of Europeans to Chinese culture and philosophy was the result, first of all, of the religious impulse exemplified by the Catholic missionaries in China, who provided the first substantive information about Chinese culture to Europe. This information was shaped by the Jesuits' realistic assessment that China was in many ways, apart from its lack of Christianity, the equal or superior of Europe. The Jesuits recognized that the Chinese, unlike those in other less technologically or materially advanced parts of the world, could not be converted by overawing them by European might. Rather, the Chinese needed to be approached as intellectual equals and shown through sophisticated argument that Christianity was in harmony with some of their most fundamental beliefs.

The Jesuits were not alone among Christian missionaries in admiring China. One of the leading critics of the Jesuits, the Spanish Dominican Domingo Navarrete (1618–1686), repeatedly said that the Chinese surpassed all other nations. Nevertheless, the Jesuits were more accommodating than other missionaries in attempting to reconcile Christianity with Chinese culture. Because the Jesuits' closest Chinese counterparts in terms of education, social standing, and moral cultivation were the Confucian literati, the Jesuits cultivated the literati and presented them in a highly favorable light to Europeans. Conversely, Buddhism and Daoism were slighted. Realizing that these teachings were less compatible with Christianity, the Jesuits presented Buddhism and Daoism in a highly unfavorable light and emphasized their negative qualities. Not until the nineteenth century would Buddhism receive more objective treatment from scholars in the West.

Since it was necessary to justify their accommodationist plan in Europe, the Jesuits worked to develop the idea that a form of natural religion existed in China. They claimed that Confucianism contained truths derived from the natural world and human reason and lacked only the truths of revelation. The dominant Jesuit view argued that most moral and social truths of Confucianism, such as honoring one's parents and treating others as we ourselves would wish to be treated, were similar to Christianity. Elements of Confucianism that conflicted with Christianity, including certain superstitious rites involving deceased ancestors and the practice of polygamy, would have to be abandoned prior to baptism. Confucius was presented as a teacher and scholar rather than a religious leader. This view led the Jesuits to undertake a Latin translation of the Confucian Four Books *(The Great Learning, Doctrine of the Mean, Analects of Confucius,* and *Mencius).* This translation project was initiated in China in the 1580s when Jesuits began using their tentative translations of these important texts as Chinese-language primers for teaching newly arrived Jesuits. These translations were handed down and improved over the years until finally they were carried back to Europe and published in a series that culminated in 1711. The most influential of these Jesuit translations was *Confucius, Philosopher of the Chinese (Confucius Sinarum Philosophus)* (Paris, 1687) (see figure 1.2). These translations were widely read in Europe and their sympathetic portrayal of Confucius was very influential.

The Jesuits succeeded in presenting Confucianism as a philosophy that was very appealing to the cultural needs of Europe in the seventeenth and eighteenth centuries. Although Confucianism lacked biblical revelation, it was otherwise complementary to Christianity and could be used to elaborate and enrich Christian teachings in the way that Greek philosophy had been used by the early church. The charity of the Chinese was compared to the charity of Christians. In fact, the reconciliation of pagan Greek and Roman authors with Christianity by Renaissance humanists provided a precedent for the reconciliation of Chinese philosophy by Christians of the seventeenth century. The Jesuits' argument was persuasive in a way that boomeranged on them. In eighteenth-century France, the teachings of Confucius were taken up by anti-Christian thinkers of the Enlightenment and used to show the admirable qualities of a philosophy that *lacked* divine revelation. The deism and benevolent despotism of Chinese monarchs seemed admirable models of what Enlightenment thinkers were promoting in Europe. Other leading European intellectuals of the time, such as the German Gottfried Wilhelm Leibniz (1646–1716), found in Confucian philosophy confirmation of universal truths that they had discovered in their own research.

The presentation of this accommodating interpretation of Confucianism became entangled with the struggle among European Christians called the Chinese Rites Controversy. The most important rites involved were rituals performed in honor of ancestors and Confucius. Some missionaries claimed that these rites involved a worship of Confucius and ancestral spirits as idols. While conceding that certain rites to ancestors were superstitions, the Jesuits argued that the rites to ancestors had an essentially social and moral significance. They did not violate the monotheistic nature of the Christian God because, the Jesuits said—although other Christians disagreed—the Chinese were not praying to their ancestors for benefits from beyond the grave. The Jesuits prohibited their converts from practicing certain rites to Confucius but allowed others on the grounds that these rites were more civil than religious.

A related debate raged over the Chinese name for God. Whereas many missionaries felt traditional Chinese terms for God, such as *Shangdi* (Lord-on-High) and *Tian* (Heaven), were tainted because they had been used in ancient, pre-Christian texts, the Jesuits used these traditional terms in an attempt to accommodate Christianity with Chinese culture. The use of the terms showed that Christianity was not alien to Chinese culture even though the meaning of the term needed to be fine-tuned to fit the exact meaning of Christianity. As an acceptable, untainted alternative, the Jesuits proposed that a new term, *Tianzhu* (Lord of Heaven), be used.

The Chinese Rites Controversy involved many people and much bitterness. Eventually the Jesuits, who were the leading proponents of accommodation, lost this battle. As a result, the Jesuit interpretation of Confucianism was discredited and accommodation was rejected by Catholic authorities in Rome in 1704, a rejection that was later confirmed by papal decrees of 1715 and 1742. (Much later, in 1939, this rejection was reversed by Rome on the grounds that Japanese Shinto rites were more civil and social than religious in nature.) Those sympathetic to Jesuit accommodation viewed the eighteenth-century rejection of accommodation as an important turning point in the history of Christianity in China. But this interpretation betrays a kind of chauvinism in that it portrays Europeans as the primary actors in this struggle and the Chinese as passive responders. The initial growth of Christianity in China in the early seventeenth century stagnated only in part because European Christians became less accommodating. The stagnation was also due to an active rejection of Christianity by Chinese on grounds that were independent of what the Europeans did. Nevertheless, the prohibition of further debate on Rites Controversy issues had a chilling effect on Confucian-Christian dialogue and, to that extent, it damaged the effort to inculturate Christianity in China.

The Proto-Sinologists

The Jesuits attempted to shape European public opinion in a way favorable to their missionary approach in China and tried to gain the support of royal or commercial patrons who would subsidize the expensive missions. The relative poverty of early modern Europe in comparison with China is shown in this preoccupation with funding. Early in the Ming dynasty, the Yongle Emperor underwrote the costs of a series of seven enormous expeditions. Some of these consisted of over three hundred ships and twenty-eight thousand men and ventured into the Indian Ocean and as far as east Africa in the years 1404–1433. Such voyages would have been impossibly beyond the means of any European monarch. One of the more elaborate European missions of the seventeenth century was the group of six Jesuits, organized in 1685 in part by the French Academy of Sciences and subsidized by Louis XIV (r. 1643–1715).

Through Europe's enthusiastic response to the Jesuits' presentations, China entered the realm of popular Western culture in the early seventeenth century. Popular culture is often grounded in less substantive concerns and so is more subject to the shifting tides of fashion, whether this involves fashionable ideas or fashionable artistic tastes. Unlike the more serious study of China by scholars of that time, the popular interest in China in the seventeenth and eighteenth centuries took the form of enthusiasms that were subject to wide and sudden swings of support.

The scholarly study of China was undertaken by a relatively small group of intellectuals. Given the commitment needed to study the Chinese language and culture, such scholars took a serious approach to China. The seventeenth-and eighteenth-century model of scholarship was that of a polyhistor (or polymath) rather than specialist. A polyhistor sought much or varied learning that included many different subjects. While the polyhistor ideal (by which scholars acquired a facility in as many fields as possible rather than expertise in only one field) may have made these scholars less specialized than today's experts, they were far from being amateurs.

The polyhistor style of scholarship culminated in Leibniz. Contemporary scholarship, which prizes expertise in a particular area of knowledge, has difficulty dealing with a polyhistor like Leibniz. The tendency is to view him as having expertise in several areas, preeminently philosophy and mathematics, but such a classification misses the point. Leibniz would have regarded such classification of his work as demeaning, because his age prized the ability to move with learned ease through as many fields as possible. Leibniz's polyhistor style of scholarship is not something easily detached from his achievements in philosophy because it could be argued (and probably would have been argued by seventeenth-century savants) that his philosophic insights were the result of the breadth of his knowledge. He worked in diverse fields, writing a history of the House of Braunschweig, directing the Herzog August Library in Wolfenbüttel, managing a Harz Mountain mine, conducting negotiations of reconciliation between Catholics and Protestants, producing a mechanical calculator, and inventing the calculus.

In order to distinguish early students of China from later China scholars, we refer to them as "proto-Sinologists." Some of their ideas about Chinese language and culture may have been false, and even ridiculous, but their interest in China was less vulnerable to the tides of intellectual fashion than the popularizers of their time. One such proto-Sinological idea was the belief in a *Clavis Sinica,* or "key" to Chinese that would enable one to radically simplify and reduce the amount of study needed to master the Chinese language. The notion of developing such a key was based upon the belief that it was possible to have a single universal language. The European discovery of many unknown languages in Asia had revived the idea of the biblical proliferation of tongues at Babel (Gen. 11:1–9), which was believed to have ended the universality of the Primitive Language given by God to Adam (Gen. 2: 19–20). One school of thought believed that once this common structure was rediscovered, the results could be applied to understanding other languages, such as Chinese. Some believed that Chinese *was* the Primitive Language that had existed prior to the confusion of tongues.

Another school of thought held that while it would be impossible to recover the Primitive Language, it would be possible to create a new universal language, using principles such as Real Characters. Real Characters involved writing that represents not merely letters or words but things and ideas. Since Real Characters are not arbitrary signs, they need not be learned but rather convey their meaning in a manner that is universally understood. Leibniz believed that the Chinese language contained Real Characters. All this was part of the seventeenth-century search for a universal language. Clearly there is a universalism operative here that may in some ways be naive but in other ways it reveals an egalitarianism (but not relativism) among cultures that predates the development of ideas about European cultural superiority.

While such a "key" to Chinese may strike us today as preposterous, it was taken seriously by many intellectuals of that time because it was reinforced by certain widely held ideas about the development of languages. Frederick William, the Great Elector of Prussia (r. 1640–1688), like many minor princes, dreamt of the wealth to be obtained through founding an East India trading company and to this end he supported proto-Sinological research. In 1674 a member of his Berlin court, the Lutheran pastor Andreas Müller (1630–1694), announced his discovery of such a key in a four-page pamphlet entitled "Proposal on a Key Suitable for Chinese" *(Propositio super clave sua Sinica)*. Müller promised to release this key upon the payment of a fee—half in advance paid into an escrow account and the remaining half upon delivery. Unfortunately, Müller's key was never revealed.

It appears that Müller's announcement of a Clavis Sinica represented a research proposal in search of funding rather than a finalized technique available for purchase. Müller's precarious position (because of theological tensions between Lutherans and Calvinists) at the Brandenburg-Berlin court, combined with the needs of supporting a large family and the frequent delay in the payment of salaries at the financially strapped court, made his demand for an advance payment less cynical than it might appear today. In addition, Müller had incurred debts in connection with producing a wooden typeset of Chinese characters. This typographia consisted of small wooden blocks upon each of which one character was engraved. These 3,284 blocks have survived and may be found in the Berlin Staatsbibliothek today. It seems that Müller had an idea for developing such a key based upon applying musical notation to reproduce the tones of the Chinese language, but his key was not yet fully developed because he needed financial support to complete it. In the understandable requests from scholars for information on his key, Müller steadfastly refused to divulge any information until the fee was paid. Just before his death, after having been discharged from his position at the Berlin court, a discouraged and embittered Müller burned his manuscripts. Yet the idea of a Clavis Sinica lived on.

The responses among European intellectuals to such a key were mixed. A prolific and well-known Jesuit scholar in Rome, Athanasius Kircher (1602–1680), was doubtful about the possibility of constructing such a key, but one of the most brilliant men of his time, Leibniz, was interested and addressed a number of questions to Müller that were never answered (and could not have been answered given the incomplete state of Müller's research). However, in 1697 when Müller's proto-Sinological successor at Berlin, the physician Christian Mentzel (1622–1701), also claimed to have developed a Clavis Sinica, Leibniz was enthusiastic. Although Mentzel's key was never presented in its entirety, several pages of it were published. They show that it was based on the lexical work of the Chinese scholar Mei Yingzuo (1570–1615) and the dictionary, *Zihui* (1615), that was organized on Mei's principles. Mei had classified the Chinese characters according to 214 radicals or classifiers (see figure 4.1). Since Chinese, lacking an alphabet, cannot be arranged in alphabetical order, these 214 radicals proved crucial in organizing and classifying the characters. However, Mentzel saw the 214-radical system as more than an artificial lexical arrangement and in fact believed that these categories revealed the underlying structure of the Chinese written language. Gradually over the seventeenth and eighteenth centuries, the meaning of a Clavis Sinica evolved from a shortcut to learning Chinese (Müller) to a translation aid (Mentzel) and finally to a Chinese grammar.

The story of the Clavis Sinica shows how far China penetrated into European culture and also teaches us that the European intellectual world of that time was far more cosmopolitan in outlook than we sometimes think. In the late seventeenth century, Brandenburg-Berlin was a political and intellectual backwater. Scholars like Müller and Mentzel were overshadowed by eminent savants like Kircher and Leibniz. Unlike Rome or Paris, Brandenburg-Berlin rarely saw a

辭源修訂本一一——四册部首目録

子 集 一 畫		女 寅	728 集	方 无 辰	1379 1396 集	生 用 田	2095 2100 2101	色 申	2610 集	草 韭 音 頁	3372 3377 3377 3381
一	1	子	773			疋疋正同	2128	艸卝同	2613	風 飛	3404 3415
丨	83	宀	799	日	1396	扩	2132	屯	2746	食首	3420
丶	93	寸	867	日	1455	癶	2149	虫	2756	香	3437
丿	97	小	882	月	1472	白	2155	血	2797		3439
乙	101	尢尣同	898	木	1493	皮	2182	行	2799		
亅	120	尸	900	欠	1651	皿	2184	衣衤同	2811	亥 集	
二 畫		屮	917	止	1661	目罒同	2197	襾	2840	十 畫	
二	122	山	918	歹	1680	矛	2225	酉 集 七 畫		馬	3443
亠	148	巛	949	殳	1687	矢	2227			骨	3471
人	158	工	952	毋	1692	石	2232	見	2852	高	3477
儿	268	己	963	比	1694	示	2262	角	2862	髟	3485
入	284	巾	966	毛	1697	内	2290	言	2872	鬥	3490
八	296	干	988	氏	1702	禾	2292	谷	2928	鬯	3492
冂	320	幺	999	气	1704	穴	2321	豆	2929	鬲	3494
冖	322	广	1003	巳 集		立	2335	豕	2934	鬼	3495
冫	325	廴	1028	水氵氺同	1707	氺同水		豸	2941	十一畫	
几	332	廾	1034	火灬同	1908	疋同正		貝	2946	魚	3502
凵	333	弋	1036	爪爫同	1965	乙同乙		赤	2976	鳥	3520
刀	337	弓	1037	爪爫同目		叩同目		走	2982	鹵	3551
力	371	彐	1059	父	1968	衤同衣		足	2991	鹿	3554
勹	385	彡	1060	爻	1969	未 集 六 畫		身	3011	麥	3561
匕	388	彳	1067	爿	1971			車	3013	麻	3564
匚	393	卩同尢		片	1972	竹	2344	辛	3037	十二畫	
匸	395	互同彐		牙	1975	米	2382	辰	3043	黃	3566
十	397	彐同彐		牛牜同	1978	糸	2394	辵辶同	3045	黍	3576
卜	430	忄同心		犬犭同	1992	缶	2478	邑右阝同	3096	黑	3577
卩	432	扌同手		攵同心		网罒冈同	2480	酉	3127	黹	3586
厂	439	氵同水		攵同火		羊	2490	釆	3143	十三畫	
厶	443	犭同犬		灬同火		羽	2502	里	3146	黽	3587
又	447	阝在右同邑		灬同爪		老	2515	戌 集 八 畫		鼎	3589
亻同人	158	阝在左同阜		王同玉		耂同老				鼓	3591
刂同刀	337	辶同辵		夗同老		而	2522	金	3155	鼠	3593
卩同卩	432	卯 集 四 畫		月同肉		耒	2523	長	3223	十四畫	
丑 集 三 畫				艹同艸		耳	2526	門	3231	鼻	3595
		心	1093	辶同辵		聿	2539	阜左阝同	3257	齊	3597
口	455	戈	1182	午 集 五 畫		肉月同	2541	隶	3300	十五畫	
囗	559	戶	1197			臣	2577	隹	3301	齒	3601
土	582	手	1203	玄	2018	自	2582	雨	3324	十六畫	
士	639	支	1331	玉王同	2027	至	2587	青	3349	龍	3605
夂	645	攴	1333	瓜	2081	臼	2590	非	3359	龜	3617
夊	645	文	1356	瓦	2084	舌	2597	九 畫		十七畫	
夕	649	斗	1367	甘	2091	舟	2600	面	3362	龠	3620
大	660	斤	1371			艮	2607	革	3364		

Fig. 4.1. The 214 radicals (classifiers) of the Chinese written language, first formulated by Mei Yingzuo (1570–1615). Reproduced from the dictionary *Ziyuan* (Shanghai, 1915; revised Beijing, 1983). The Chinese written language is not based upon an alphabet, and these radicals have been the primary basis for organizing characters in Chinese dictionaries during the past four hundred years.

missionary from China. And yet the Great Elector Frederick William had great hopes for his kingdom, and China was viewed as having a part in that greatness. Consequently, the Great Elector encouraged the work of proto-Sinologists like Müller and Mentzel to gather information on China's language, geography, botany, medicines, history, and literature. As a result, an impressive early collection of Chinese books was amassed in Berlin along with Müller's typographia of Chinese characters on wooden blocks.

Additional evidence for the lack of European cultural superiority in the seventeenth century is shown by the intellectual challenge that China's history posed to European identity. Whereas theology was known as the queen of the sciences in Europe, in China this role was occupied by history. China's historical experience as the longest continuous civilization in the world has fostered a historical scholarship unparalleled in any other culture. Seventeenth-century Europe had a passion for precise chronologies and that passion was inevitably tied to the Bible. In 1650–1654 in London, the Anglican archbishop James Ussher published a chronology in Latin entitled *Annals of the Old and New Testaments* in which he dated the creation of Adam to 4004 B.C. and the Noachian flood to 2349 B.C. Ussher's dates became so widely accepted that they were inserted into the margins of reference editions of the King James version of the Bible.

Less than ten years after the publication of Ussher's book, the Jesuit missionary Martino Martini returned from China and published the first edition in Latin of his work on Chinese history, *The First Ten Divisions of Chinese History (Sinicae historiae decas prima res)* (Munich, 1658). This was the first genuine history of China to appear in a European language (though it concluded at 1 B.C.). Drawing from Chinese historical records, Martini dated the beginning of Chinese history from Fu Xi in 2952 B.C. He also followed Chinese scholars in eliminating numerous legendary events, including several creation myths. Anti-Jesuit feeling in Europe was so strong that some Europeans dismissed China's historical longevity as a myth created by the Jesuits for their own ends; however, many others accepted the claim of China's high antiquity.

The challenge to Ussher's chronology that Martini's book raised was immediately apparent. In the seventeenth-century biblical view of human history, Noah was the father of all mankind because everyone, apart from Noah and his descendants, was thought to have been killed at the time of the Flood. However, if the Chinese could trace their history from a point in time before the Flood, then the claim of Noah's universal patriarchy was destroyed because there would have been another line of human descent. If the Flood did not occur until 2349 B.C. and if the Chinese could date their history from 2952 B.C., then either Noah was not the father of mankind or one of the chronologies was wrong.

Martini and others immediately saw the solution, but it required a change in the biblical dating. Ussher's dates were supported by the fourth-century Vulgate version of the Bible, which was a Latin translation by Saint Jerome (ca. 347–420?) based on now lost Hebrew texts. However, there was an older translation of the Old Testament, the Septuagint, a Greek translation allegedly made by seventy-two scholars at Alexandria under the reign of Ptolemy Philadelphus (285–246 B.C.). One biblical chronology suggested by the Septuagint placed the Creation at 5200 B.C. and the Flood at 2957 B.C., or five years prior to the beginning of Chinese history in 2952 B.C. Adopting this dating would preserve Noah's universal patrimony. Although debate would continue over the dating of biblical events, the debate shows how European culture was intellectually challenged by China. In the process, Chinese history was integrated into European "universal history" based on Old Testament–derived chronologies.

The way in which Jesuit publications on China, such as Martini's history, influenced European popular culture is shown in the case of John Webb (1611–1672) of England. Webb was an architect and antiquarian who published a book entitled *An Historical Essay Endeavoring a Probability that the Language of the Empire of China Is the Primitive Language* (London, 1669). Although he did not seriously study the Chinese language, Webb did read widely in the books on China, mainly by Jesuits, published in Europe, and he attempted to reconcile biblical and Chinese history. Webb claimed that the descendants of Noah (specifically, the descendants of Shem, one of Noah's three sons) had migrated to China and thereby had preserved the Primitive Language. On the basis of the parallels Martini had drawn between the biblical flood and the flood said to have occurred in China during the time of King Yao, Webb hypothesized that Noah and Yao were identical and that the Flood was worldwide.

Leibniz, Bouvet, and Figurism

Leibniz stands out as a monumental European figure whose understanding of Chinese culture was remarkably sophisticated for his age. He not only avidly read the books on China published in Europe but he also initiated direct contact, mainly through correspondence, with Jesuits in China. In his famous introduction to *The Latest News of China (Novissima Sinica)* (1697), Leibniz wrote that Europeans surpassed the Chinese in the contemplative sciences and were the equals of the Chinese in technology. However, he said that Europeans were, in turn, surpassed by the Chinese in practical philosophy, by which he meant the adaptation of ethics and politics to contemporary life. Leibniz feared that Europe would be at a disadvantage to China if the exchange of missionaries between the two countries were not reciprocal. He advocated that Christian missionaries to China who taught revealed religion to the Chinese should be counterbalanced by missionaries from China who would teach Europeans the practice of natural religion.

Of Leibniz's correspondence, the most intellectually fruitful was with the Frenchman Joachim Bouvet, S.J. (1656–1730). Father Bouvet was one of the outstanding missionaries of the late seventeenth and early eighteenth centuries. He first arrived in China in 1687, as part of the group of French Jesuits who had been equipped by the French Academy of Sciences with scientific instruments to be used in China. Sponsored by the greatest monarch in Europe, Louis XIV,

Bouvet was selected by the greatest monarch in Asia, the Kangxi Emperor, to reside at the court in Beijing. In 1693 Bouvet returned to Europe at the request of the Kangxi Emperor to cultivate ties with Louis XIV and to recruit more Jesuits, whose mathematical and scientific skills were valued at the Chinese court. While in Europe, Bouvet published an extremely favorable, even hagiographical, work on the Kangxi Emperor entitled *Portrait historique de l'Empereur de la Chine* (Paris, 1697) and dedicated the work to Louis XIV. Just before returning to China in 1697, Bouvet wrote a letter to Leibniz that initiated one of the most remarkable correspondences of that time.

Whereas Ricci and the Jesuits who followed his accommodation method and concentrated on translating the Confucian Four Books had extensive contact with Chinese literati in the provinces as well as in the capital, Bouvet's circles were far more limited to the court at Beijing, which since 1644 had been dominated by Manchus. His proximity to the Kangxi Emperor (he tutored the emperor in geometry) and the imperial support he received gave Bouvet's powerful creativity free play in developing a striking but very controversial theory about the relationship of Christianity to the Chinese classics.

Bouvet was far more interested in the older Chinese classics, the Five Classics *(Book of Changes, Book of Odes, Book of Documents, Record of Rites,* and *Spring and Autumn Annals),* than in the Four Books. Earlier Jesuits, including Ricci, had accepted the dominant Chinese literati viewpoint in interpreting the Chinese classics as historical texts whose contents were to be interpreted literally. Ricci had argued that these texts revealed that the Chinese had developed natural religion, that is, moral truths about right and wrong that were discernible through human reason and without divine revelation. However, Bouvet's analysis convinced him that Chinese characters were hieroglyphs (picture writing) that should be interpreted figuratively. This led Bouvet to conclude that the Chinese classics should be interpreted, not literally as historical texts, but figuratively as allegorical texts. He interpreted the book of Genesis to mean that the Chinese were descended from a biblical people who had been dispersed to East Asia. The Chinese had preserved in their written script the hieroglyphic language of biblical antiquity.

According to Bouvet, the Chinese chronologies were wrong in claiming Fu Xi (2952 B.C.) as the historical founder of China. Bouvet agreed with Chinese historians of his own day who regarded Fu Xi as a mythical figure and began Chinese history six centuries later with the three sage rulers, Yao, Shun, and Yu. According to Bouvet, Fu Xi was not Chinese but rather the universal lawgiver of all ancient civilizations who was known in different ancient texts by different names. The ancient Egyptians and Greeks referred to him as Hermes (or Mercurius) Trismegistus; the Hellenistic culture of Alexandria called him Thoth; the Arabs called him Edris or Adris; and the Hebrews called him Enoch. This universal lawgiver gave to these ancient peoples laws, customs, religion, science, letters, language, and books. In addition, Bouvet claimed that this divine wisdom had survived among ancient Egyptian priests, Chaldean magi, Pythagoreans, Socrates, Platonists, Gallic Druids, Indian Brahmans, and Chinese followers of Confucius and Laozi (i.e., early and purer, not later and corrupted Daoists). Actually, Bouvet belonged to a tradition of Christian apologists called the Ancient Theology (*prisca theologia*) of Hermetism (after Hermes Trismegistus), which maintained that certain pagan writings foreshadowed Christ's revelation. Because of this emphasis on a figurative interpretation of the Chinese classics, Bouvet and his followers were called Figurists and his theory was called Figurism.

Ricci, in his accommodation theory, had claimed that the ancient Chinese had developed a form of monotheism and natural religion that had since been corrupted by Buddhist and Neo-Confucian influences. The Figurists were much more radical than Ricci in claiming that the most ancient Chinese classics contained in allegorical and symbolical form anticipations of New Testament teachings and Christ's revelation. Figurism was such a radical theory that even Jesuits were reluctant to accept it. The Rites Controversy would force the Jesuits to completely repudiate the theory as too radical. Ironically, recent Sinological research has echoed some of Bouvet's fundamental claims that the Chinese classical texts, at least some of the older texts, should be interpreted as figurative rather than historical texts.

The Jesuit accommodation embodied in the production of *Confucius Sinarum Philosophus* had focused on Confucius and the classics most closely associated with his name, namely, the Four Books. Bouvet's accommodation, by contrast, avoided dealing with Confucius and concentrated on the Five Classics, which were produced prior to the time of Confucius (551–ca. 479 B.C.) but supposedly later edited by Confucius. Of the Five Classics, Bouvet concentrated on what is regarded by many as the oldest extant Chinese text, the *Book of Changes (Yijing)*. In response to Leibniz's questions about finding a key to the Chinese language of the sort that Andreas Müller sought, Bouvet revealed that he too was a believer in the notion of the Primitive Language, or the writing used before the Flood. Furthermore, he believed that the characters of the *Book of Changes* could reveal this universal language.

Bouvet believed that the diagrams attributed to Fu Xi in the *Book of Changes* contained vestiges of the knowledge of the most ancient human beings. However, he claimed that Confucius and his followers had confused and obscured the original meaning. Bouvet believed that only by laying aside the Confucian commentarial tradition and examining Fu Xi's diagrams mathematically could the true meaning of the diagrams be discovered. In short, Fu Xi's diagrams revealed a mystical mathematical vision that could make rational the works of God by reducing everything to the quantitative elements of number, weight, and measure. Bouvet believed that Fu Xi's mystical mathematical vision, which included music, was similar to that of the ancient Greek secret society of Pythagoras (ca. 582–ca. 500 B.C.), which attempted to explain the world through the mysteries of mathematics and music. Leibniz's mathematics confirmed Bouvet in his thinking.

In their correspondence, Bouvet and Leibniz made one of the most remarkable discoveries in the Western encounter with China. Leibniz had developed a binary system of arithmetic, which, unlike the commonly used denary system of today that relies upon ten digits (0, 1, 2, 3, 4, 5, 6, 7, 8, and 9), generated all arithmetical calculations using only two numbers (0 and 1). If we were to compare the denary and binary systems, 0 in the denary system equals 0 in the binary system and 1 in the denary system equals 1 in the binary system. The denary 3 equals 11 in the binary system, 4 = 100, 5 = 101, 6 = 110, 7 = 111, 8 = 1000, 9 = 100l, 10 = 1010, 32 = 100000, 62 = 111110, and 63 = 111111.

When Leibniz sent an explanation of his binary system to Bouvet, Bouvet responded by sending him an arrangement of the diagrams of the *Book of Changes* that showed astounding similarities to his binary system. The diagrams of the *Book of Changes* are all reducible to two fundamental elements: a whole line (called *yang*) and a broken line (called *yin*). The *Book of Changes* contains sixty-four six-lined figures, or hexagrams. Each of the lines of a hexagram is either broken or whole. Bouvet noted that if each broken line were regarded as equivalent to 0 and if each whole line were regarded as equivalent to 1, then an arrangement of the sixty-four hexagrams corresponded perfectly to Leibniz's binary progression. As applied to the sixty-four hexagrams of the *Book of Changes*, the equivalences would be as follows:

denary system	binary system
0	0
1	1
2	01
3	11
4	100
5	101
6	110
7	111
8	1000
9	1001
10	1010
...	...
32	100000
...	...
62	111110
63	111111

In his letter to Leibniz written from Beijing on 4 November 1701, Bouvet enclosed a copy of the A Priori (Natural, Original) Hexagram Order *(Xiantian Zixu)* in which the sixty-four hexagrams are arranged in a rectangular and a circular order (see figure 4.2). After receiving this diagram, Leibniz inscribed in his distinctive handwriting arabic numbers alongside each of the hexagrams to show their equivalents in the denary system. For example, the hexagram in the upper left of the rectangular arrangement consists of six broken lines, which in the binary system would represent 000000 or simply 0. The hexagram to its immediate right represents one whole line on top and five broken lines below, which in the binary system would represent 000001 or 1. The next hexagram on the

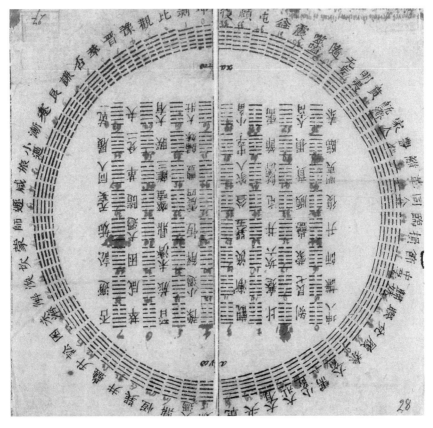

Fig. 4.2. The A Priori (Natural) Hexagram Order *(Xiantian Zixu)* containing the sixty-four hexagrams of the *Book of Changes (Yijing)*, sent by the Jesuit Father Joachim Bouvet to Leibniz in 1701. The (denary) numerical equivalents have been inscribed by Leibniz's own hand at the top of each hexagram. Courtesy of the Leibniz Archiv, Niedersächsische Landesbibliothek, Hannover.

immediate right consists of one broken line on top, one whole line immediately below, and four broken lines below that, which in the binary system would represent 000010 or in the denary system 2. Finally, moving to the last hexagram in the lower right of the rectangular arrangement, one finds six whole lines, which in the binary system would represent 111111 or in the denary system 63.

Leibniz took certain liberties with the system, such as counting the lines from the top to bottom rather than in the traditional Chinese manner of counting from bottom to top. In addition, this is only one of several forms in which the hexagrams are arranged; in the other arrangements, they would not reflect such a perfect binary progression. Nevertheless, these points do not invalidate the remarkable similarities. Bouvet was impressed by the fact that Leibniz's "numerical calculus" reduced counting and creation to a common mathematical basis. Bouvet believed that Leibniz had rediscovered a system that had been discovered by the Chinese in antiquity. That the greatest mind in Europe of his day had reproduced the system of the Chinese ancients confirmed their a priori nature and his figuristic interpretation of the Chinese classics. Leibniz, for his part, believed that this diagram from ancient China confirmed his notion of Real Characters and his mathematical vision by which he saw part of the principle by which God had created the universe. We live in an age that has gone so far in relativizing truth into a function of a given culture (one culture's truths being as valid as those of any other) that the visions of Leibniz and Bouvet, who saw truth as universal and absolute, are difficult for us to grasp.

The European View of the Literati Tradition: Confucianism versus Neo-Confucianism

The transfer of ideas from China to Europe is one of the most fascinating but difficult trails for historians to follow. It also reveals how certain ideas of Chinese culture were selected for transfer while others were rejected. In order to advance their program of accommodation between Christianity and Chinese culture, the Jesuits not only deemphasized and criticized Buddhism and Daoism but also were selective in their use of Confucianism. They promoted the aspects of Confucianism that were most complementary to Christianity while criticizing those aspects that they deemed incompatible.

Confucianism began as a teaching that revered Chinese antiquity and the sages. The wisdom of these sages was transmitted in the classics, edited by Confucius. As the years passed, the Confucian teaching expanded to include a reverence for the family and ancestors, an imperial ideology, a cosmology that linked the cosmos with human affairs, the examination system by which officials were chosen on the basis of merit rather than birth, and a tradition of moral and spiritual cultivation. The famous illustration of Confucius presented by the Jesuits to Europeans in 1687 (see figure 1.2) depicted Confucius as a scholar-sage in a library rather than as a god or prophet in a temple. This depiction shows how the Jesuits emphasized the rational side of Confucianism that became prevalent in Europe.

It is important to note that the term "Confucianism" has no equivalent in China. The term was invented by the Jesuits and reflected a distinctly Jesuit interpretation of this important school of Chinese philosophy. It represents a Latinization of the Chinese name by which "Kong-fu-zi" (Master Kong) became "Confucius," first presented to Europeans in 1687 in the influential work *Confucius Sinarum Philosophus*. (The name of only one other Chinese philosopher was widely Latinized by the Jesuits in this way, namely, Mengzi [ca. 372–289 B.C.], who became Mencius.) The Chinese referred to this school as the Literati Teaching *(Ru Jiao)* because they believed that the school began long before Confucius. Confucius himself acknowledged this in claiming that he was a transmitter and not a creator *(Analects* 7:1). Confucius was not merely being modest here but was absolutely sincere in his belief that he was simply transmitting the Truth *(Dao)* of the ancients. Of course, this Truth was a developing philosophy that Confucius shaped through editing the classical texts. And yet because he did not compose the classics from scratch, it is misleading to name this school of philosophy after Confucius. The Jesuits named the school after him, not because of a misunderstanding, but because they were trying to give a certain emphasis to parts of this Literati Teaching that were contained in the Four Books.

The history of this Literati Teaching (Confucianism) might be divided into two major phases (early and later) separated by a long intervening period around A.D. 220–960, which roughly paralleled the early Middle Ages in Europe. During this intermediary seven-hundred-year period, Confucianism went into steep decline while Buddhism and Daoism flourished. When Confucianism revived in the tenth century, cosmological and metaphysical dimensions were absorbed through the influence of Buddhism and Daoism. The Jesuits were not the only Western interpreters of China who used new terminology to explain Chinese culture. Whereas most Chinese scholars emphasized the continuity of the literati tradition, Western scholars have emphasized its discontinuity. This is reflected in Western scholars' use of the terms "classical Confucianism" and "Neo-Confucianism" (which have no equivalents in Chinese) to refer to the early and later phases.

Ricci was the most influential voice in shaping the early Jesuit approach in China. Ricci and his followers argued that the Confucianism prior to A.D. 220 had been a truer form of philosophy than the revived Confucianism after 960. The Jesuits, in *Confucius Sinarum Philosophus,* referred to these later Confucians as "Modern Interpreters" *(Neoterici Interpretes);* by 1777 the term had evolved into "Neo-Confucians" *(les néo-confuciens).* According to the Jesuits, these Neo-Confucians had been corrupted by the influence of Buddhism from India. Chinese philosophers were aware that the later form of Confucianism had additional elements not found in the earlier form, but they did not see the degree of discontinuity that the Jesuits saw. The Chinese tended to see these additions as part of a tradition of continuous accretions to the same essential form of Confucianism. In their view, these accretions developed rather than distorted the philosophy, although there was debate among Chinese scholars about specific accretions being undesirable because they carried the tradition off in a direction not intended by the ancients. Most of the missionaries viewed Neo-Confucian cosmology and metaphysics as philosophically materialistic and atheistic and so they preferred to emphasize the Confucianism of the earlier period, which lacked many of these materialistic and atheistic elements.

Not all Europeans agreed with this negative assessment of Neo-Confucianism. Leibniz, for example, was fascinated by the Neo-Confucian philosophy and some believe he was influenced by it. The late English historian of science Joseph Needham, in the second volume (1956) of his *Science and Civilisation in China,* claimed that the philosophy of organism entered into European history from China by way of Leibniz. One of the most distinctive aspects of Leibnizian philosophy is its theory of the monads. According to this theory, all elements of the world are reducible to units called "monads." These monads act, not because of any causal interaction with other elements, but because of some internal programming that has been coordinated by the creator God to guarantee that the monads interact with one another in harmony. God's advance programming of the monads to ensure their harmonious interaction is called the "preestablished harmony," and Needham believed that Leibniz was influenced in the development of this theory by the Neo-Confucian philosophy of Zhu Xi (1130–1200).

The unfolding of the Leibnizian monads not by reacting with one another but rather by a cosmic resonance is remarkably similar to the organic worldview of Neo-Confucianism. This philosophy of organism was based upon correlative thinking, which assumes that there is a fundamental correspondence between the cosmic patterns of the natural world and patterns of the human world and moral sphere. This preestablished correspondence guarantees a natural harmony. While the chronological development of Leibniz's philosophy contradicts the claim that he received the idea of monads from his study of Chinese Neo-Confucianism, it is clear that Leibniz did at least receive important confirmation for his theories from China and that this confirmation may have contributed to his further development of the philosophy of organism.

Influence of Chinese Art upon European Artists

Just as European art influenced Chinese artists in indirect ways and served as a stimulus for some of the most creative Chinese painters, so too did Chinese art stimulate the creativity of European artists. However, whereas in China the influence was not openly acknowledged and indeed appears to have been unconsciously expressed, in Europe the influence was widely acknowledged. A fashionable craving for things Chinese was led by the "apes [imitators] of China" *(magots de la Chine)*. This craving produced an imaginative hybrid art form referred to by the French word "chinoiserie" (pronounced: sheen-<u>waz</u>-eh-ree) that blended Chinese and European elements. It combined Chinese subject motifs with European rococo (pronounced ro-<u>ko</u>-ko) style and was especially appropriate for highly decorated textiles and porcelains. While chinoiserie appeared distinctly Chinese to European eyes, Chinese viewers would have had difficulty recognizing this art as their own.

The greatest Chinese influence was felt in European porcelains. Chinese ceramics were so technically and aesthetically superior that traditional European stoneware lost its appeal. Chinese porcelain began to be exported to Europe in the seventeenth century on a vast scale. By the eighteenth century the two-hundred-ship fleet of the Dutch East India Company was carrying tens of millions of pieces of Chinese porcelain to Europe. Chinese artisans produced export porcelain based on designs modeled on what they believed to be European aesthetic taste, and the hybrid forms were striking. Meanwhile Europeans began to develop European porcelain centers on Chinese models, including the high-temperature kilns established at Meissen, Saxony, in 1709. The result was that porcelain production saw the greatest degree of interaction between Chinese and Europeans of any art form.

Sino-Western interchange in other art forms was more subtle. The first European to produce engravings based on Chinese models was Johann Neuhof. Neuhof had accompanied a Dutch embassy to Beijing in 1656 and after returning to Europe, he produced a book at Amsterdam in 1665 with 150 illustrations, *An Embassy from the East India Company of the United Provinces to the Emperor of China*. The demand for Neuhof's book was so great that the French text was translated into Dutch, German, English, and Latin and was widely distributed. A second book that had a tremendous influence on shaping the European image of China was *China Illustrata* (Amsterdam, 1667) by Athanasius Kircher, S.J., who was one of the most famous scholars of seventeenth-century Europe. Although Kircher had not personally visited China, he edited the reports of fellow Jesuits who had lived there. Of the many engravings in *China Illustrata*, several are based on Chinese paintings and woodcuts brought from Beijing by Father Johann Grueber. According to the art historian Michael Sullivan, one

Fig. 4.3. Possibly the first presentation of a Chinese landscape painting (in the scroll on the table) in Europe, an engraving from Athanasius Kircher, S.J., *China Illustrata* (Amsterdam, 1667), between pages 114 and 115.

illustration, of a palace woman holding a bird and inscribed by the character *tiao* (framed above her head, meaning beautiful and refined, in the sense of a secluded woman), contains the first representation of a Chinese landscape painting in European art (see figure 4.3). This illustration is a rare example among Western prints in which a Chinese painting played a significant role.

Fig. 4.4. An engraving commemorating the Manchu victory over the Kashgarites at the Black River in 1758, made in Paris in 1771 by J. Ph. Le Bas based upon a drawing made in 1765 in China by the Jesuit Father G. Castiglione. Plate 7 in a series of sixteen, 17005, Musée Guimet, Paris. ©Photo RMN (Réunion des musées nationaux)–Ravaux. This series was produced at the instigation of the Qianlong Emperor to commemorate Manchu victories over the Dzungars and Kashgarites in eastern Turkestan that led to the annexation of Xinjiang to China in 1759.

The most notable example of Sino-Western collaboration on the production of a set of engravings dates from the Qianlong Emperor's wish to commemorate Manchu victories over the Dzungars and Kashgarites in the 1750s. These victories led to the absorption of the northwestern border region of Xinjiang into the Chinese empire. The emperor commissioned four Jesuit artists (Fathers G. Castiglione, J. D. Attiret, Jean-Damascene Salusti, and I. Sichelbarth) who were in residence at the court in Beijing to prepare sixteen drawings of battle scenes. These drawings were prepared around 1765 and were sent to Paris, where copper etchings were prepared at the Qianlong Emperor's expense by the French engraver J. Ph. Le Bas (1707–1783) and others from 1767 through 1774. The sixteen engraved plates arrived in Beijing over the years 1769–1775. (See figure 4.4.) Before the plates were returned to China, Louis XIV and some court aristocrats and Sinophiles obtained copies of the engravings. From these copies, a student of Le Bas named Isadore Stanislas Helman in 1785 produced a condensed album of engravings of the battle scenes for a curious French public.

In contrast with porcelain, very few examples of Chinese paintings found their way to Europe. Those that did were produced by professional artists rather than the literati gentlemen artists who at the time were producing the best paintings in China. In fact, most of the examples of Chinese painting that circulated in

Europe were painted on porcelain as decoration and, consequently, its quality was not likely to impress European painters. The paintings that were brought to Rome did not circulate widely outside of Italy. Most of the examples of Chinese painting came through Dutch and French trading companies. The French East India Company was founded in 1660 and by 1700 substantial numbers of Chinese painted folding screens were circulating in France, along with hand-printed wallpaper and paintings on paper. This Chinese artwork was prized for its exotic qualities, but as examples of Chinese painting, they were not remarkable.

At the end of the seventeenth century, King Louis XIV and the Kangxi Emperor exchanged gifts that included illustrated books from China. Using the examples of Chinese art in circulation in France, well-known artists such as Antoine Watteau (1684–1721), François Boucher (1703–1770)—the favorite painter of Louis XV's mistress, Madame de Pompadour—and Jean-Honoré Fragonard (1732–1806) specialized in rococo painting. Watteau, who may have owned Chinese paintings, painted pictures that attempted to reproduce the Chinese style. Although they were accepted by his European audience as being faithful to the Chinese style, in retrospect we see that the differences were great enough to justify referring to them as examples of the completely new and

Fig. 4.5. The ritual plowing of the earth performed each spring by the Chinese emperor, in an engraving by I. S. Helman of Paris, 1786. Plate 17 from the album by Helman preserved in the Musée Guimet, Paris. ©Photo RMN (Réunion des musées nationaux)–Ravaux. This rite was admired by the philosophes and emulated by certain enlightened despots of eighteenth-century Europe.

hybrid Sino-Western style, chinoiserie. During the eighteenth century, there was a rage for birds and flowers painted in this pseudo-Chinese style.

During the eighteenth century, the enthusiasm for China and its culture (Sinomania) caused certain elements of Chinese culture to be absorbed into Europe. One was the ritual plowing of the earth performed by the Chinese emperor every spring (see figure 4.5). Voltaire praised the rite and monarchs imitated it, including Louis XV in 1756. An engraving done about 1770 depicts the future Louis XVI performing the ritual plowing, and an etching records the ceremonial plowing that Emperor Joseph II of Austria performed in 1769.

There was very little contact between European painters who worked in the Chinese court and those who worked in Europe. One missionary painter who returned to Europe was the Neapolitan Matteo Ripa (see chapter 3). The rare European painters who visited China outside of missionary auspices had little contact with Chinese painters. One notable example was the English painter William Alexander (1767–1816), who accompanied the embassy of Lord Macartney to the Qianlong Emperor's court in 1792–1794. Apart from his Chinese subject matter, Alexander's art appears to have been untouched by this contact with China and remained distinctly European.

The appearance of Chinese art in Europe caused a fundamental change in aesthetic tastes. One may debate how accurately Europeans of this time understood Chinese art—clearly chinoiserie was not the same as Chinese art—but the change in European aesthetic tastes was real. The classical style, which had emphasized that beauty was the result of regularity, uniformity, simplicity, and balance (i.e., that beauty was geometrical), gave way to new aesthetic standards that prized irregularity, asymmetry, variety, and delightful complexity. Although cultural causes for such a change are complex and difficult to define fully, it is clear that the admiration for Chinese gardens played an important role.

This movement had particular application in England, where it became part of the emergence of a broad cultural movement known as romanticism. The English garden took on many of the characteristics attributed to Chinese gardens. One of the leading proponents of this movement was Sir William Temple, who in an essay *Upon Heroick Virtue* (1683) spoke of the irregular nature of beauty in Chinese gardens. To make his point, Temple used a word *sharawadgi* (meaning picturesque), which he attributed to the Chinese but which was in fact an invented word of pure chinoiserie, that is, a European word created under the inspiration of China. Later Joseph Addison, writing in *Spectator* (no. 414, 25 June 1712), elaborated and further developed Temple's ideas by saying that the landscape of Chinese gardens tended to resemble natural landscape and was free of the artificial geometrical qualities found in seventeenth-century French gardens. Rather, Chinese gardens were ungeometrical, irregular, varied (rather than simple), and without a clearly intelligible plan.

The enthusiasm for Chinese gardens continued until 1772, when the Sinophile Sir William Chambers attempted to correct some of the excesses of chinoiserie in his *Dissertation on Oriental Gardening*. Chambers argued that the aim of Chinese gardens was not to imitate nature or anything else but rather to express and evoke passions and powerful sensations. Clearly, Chambers was anticipating the movement of romanticism here. To this end, Chambers introduced some highly artificial (i.e., unnatural) elements in improving the Kew Gardens, the most famous of which was a ten-tiered Chinese pagoda, which was widely imitated throughout Europe. He also introduced at Kew a pavilion decorated with panels depicting the life of Confucius. However, by detaching the aim of the Chinese garden from an attempt to re-create nature, Chambers made the style more vulnerable to the shifting tides of cultural fashion. Because of the superficiality on which the enthusiasm for chinoiserie was founded, it is not surprising that it was short-lived not only in England but also in France, where both chinoiserie and the rococo style were overwhelmed by the French Revolution of 1789 and its return to classicism.

Works Consulted

Appleton, William. *A Cycle of Cathay: The Chinese Vogue in England during the Seventeenth and Eighteenth Centuries.* New York: Columbia University Press, 1951.

Barzin, Germain. *Baroque and Rococo.* Translated from the French by Jonathan Griffin. London: Thames & Hudson, 1964.

Bodde, Derk. "Myths of Ancient China." In *Mythologies of the Ancient World,* edited by Samuel Noah Kramer, 367–408. Garden City, N.Y.: Doubleday, 1961.

Ching, Julia, and Willard G. Oxtoby. *Moral Enlightenment: Leibniz and Wolff on China.* Nettetal, Germany: Steyler, 1992.

Collani, Claudia. *P. Joachim Bouvet S.J., sein Leben und sein Werk.* Nettetal, Germany: Steyler, 1985.

———, ed. *Vorschlag einer wissenschaftlichen Akademie für China: Briefe des Chinamissionars Joachim Bouvet S.J. an Gottfried Wilhelm Leibniz und an Jean-Paul Bignon [aus dem Jahre 1704].* Stuttgart: Franz Steiner, 1989.

Cummins, J. S. *A Question of Rites: Friar Domingo Navarrete and the Jesuits in China.* Aldershot, England: Scolar, 1993.

Dawson, Raymond. *The Chinese Chameleon: An Analysis of European Conceptions of Chinese Civilization.* London: Oxford University Press, 1967.

Hao, Zhenhua, "The Historical Circumstances and Significance of Castiglione's War Paintings of the Qianlong Emperor's Campaign against the Dzungars in the Northwestern Border Region" (in Chinese). *Sino-Western Cultural Relations Journal* 13 (1991): 18–32.

Hudson, G. F. "China and the World: A Summary of Intellectual and Artistic Influences." In *Legacy of China,* edited by Raymond Dawson. London: Oxford University Press, 1964.

Jensen, Lionel. *Manufacturing Confucianism: Chinese Traditions and Universal Civiliza-tion.* Durham, N.C.: Duke University Press, 1997.

Kircher, Athanasius. *China Illustrata.* Translated by Charles D. Van Tuyl from the 1677 original Latin edition. Muskegee, Okla.: Indian University Press, 1987.

Lach, Donald F. *Asia in the Making of Europe.* Vol. 2, *A Century of Wonder,* bks. 2 and 3. (Chicago: University of Chicago Press, 1977. In collaboration with Edwin J. Van Kley, vol. 3: *A Century of Advance,* bk. 4, *East Asia.* 1993.

———. *Preface to Leibniz' Novissima Sinica.* Honolulu: University of Hawaii Press, 1957.

Ledderose, Lothar. "Chinese Influence on European Art, Sixteenth to Eighteenth Cen-turies." In *China and Europe: Images and Influences in Sixteenth to Eighteenth Centuries,* edited by Thomas H. C. Lee, 221–49. Hong Kong: Chinese University Press, 1991.

Legouix, Susan. *The Image of China: William Alexander.* London: Jupiter, 1980.

Leibniz, Gottfried Wilhelm. *Writings on China.* Translated by Daniel J. Cook and Henry Rosemont Jr. Chicago: Open Court, 1994.

Loehr, George. "Peking-Jesuit Missionary-Artist Drawings Sent to Paris in the Eighteenth Century." *Gazette des Beaux-Arts* 60 (October 1962): 419–28.

Lovejoy, Arthur O. "The Chinese Origin of Romanticism." In *Essays in the History of Ideas,* edited by Arthur O. Lovejoy, 99–135. Baltimore: Johns Hopkins University Press, 1948.

Lundbæk, Knud. "The Establishment of European Sinology, 1801–1815." In *Cultural Encounters: Japan, China and the West,* edited by S. Clausen et al. Aarhus, Denmark: Aarhus University Press, 1995. 15–54.

———. "Notes sur l'image du Neó-Confucianisme dans la littérature europeéne du dix-septième à la fin du dix-neuvième siècle." In *Actes du troisième Colloque international de sinologie. Chantilly 1980,* 131–76. Paris: Belles Lettres, 1983.

Minamiki, George. *The Chinese Rites Controversy from Its Beginnings to Modern Times.* Chicago: Loyola University Press, 1985.

Mungello, D. E. *Curious Land: Jesuit Accommodation and the Origins of Sinology.* Stuttgart: Franz Steiner, 1985.

———. "European Philosophical Responses to Non-European Culture: China." In *The Cambridge History of Seventeenth-Century Philosophy,* edited by Daniel Garber and Michael Ayers, 87–100. Cambridge: Cambridge University Press, 1998.

———. *Leibniz and Confucianism: The Search for Accord.* Honolulu: University of Hawaii Press, 1977.

Needham, Joseph. *Science and Civilization in China.* Vol. 2, *History of Scientific Thought.* Cambridge: Cambridge University Press, 1956.

Pelliot, Paul. "Les 'Conquêtes de l'empereur de la Chine,'" *T'oung Pao* 20 (1921): 183–274.

Reichwein, Adolf. *China and Europe: Intellectual and Artistic Contacts in the Eighteenth Century.* Translated by J. C. Powell. London: Kegan Paul, 1925.

Rowbotham, Arnold H. "The Impact of Confucianism on Seventeenth-Century Europe." *Far Eastern Quarterly* 4 (1944): 224–42.

Rule, Paul A. *K'ung-tzu or Confucius? The Jesuit Interpretation of Confucianism.* Sydney: Allen & Unwin, 1986.

Sullivan, Michael. *The Meeting of Eastern and Western Art from the Sixteenth Centuy to the Present Day.* New York: New York Graphic Society, 1973.

Van Kley, Edwin J. "Europe's 'Discovery' of China and the Writing of World History." *American Historical Review* 76 (April 1971): 358–85.

Wills, John E., Jr. *Pepper, Guns, and Parleys: The Dutch East India Company at China, 1662–1681.* Cambridge: Harvard University Press, 1974.

Witek, John W. *Controversial Ideas in China and Europe: A Biography of Jean-François Foucquet, S.J. (1665–1741).* Rome: Institutum Historicum Societatis Iesu, 1982.

Wittkower, Rudolf. "English Neo-Palladianism, the Landscape Garden, China, and the Enlightenment," *L'Arte* (Milan) 6 (June 1969): 18–35.

5

European Rejection of Chinese Culture and Confucianism

China Popularizers in Europe

To appreciate the different depths to which China penetrated the cultural interests of Europe in the seventeenth and eighteenth centuries, it is important to distinguish three levels of Europeans who studied and published books on China. The first level consisted of missionaries, mainly Jesuits, who had years of firsthand experience in China studying the difficult Chinese language and making contact with the Chinese.

The second level consisted of proto-Sinologists, who had a serious but less focused interest in China than the missionaries. Many of the proto-Sinologists believed in some common, universal basis of languages. This led, in the seventeenth century, to the belief that Chinese was perhaps the biblical Primitive Language that existed prior to the multiplication of tongues at Babel or Leibniz's view that Chinese contained Real Characters that could communicate on a universal scale. Other proto-Sinologists postulated some remarkable similarities between Chinese and several eastern Mediterranean languages and cultures. However, they had a Middle Eastern bias that led them to see knowledge spreading from the Middle East to China rather than the reverse. For example, the most prolific polyhistor of his age was the German-born Jesuit Athanasius Kircher of Rome. Kircher believed that Egyptian culture had been disseminated to China through Noah's son Ham (rather than Shem or Japheth) (Genesis 10) and, as a result, the Egyptian hieroglyphs were more ancient, purer, and deeper in hidden meaning than the Chinese characters. Kircher and other so-called disseminationists were too rooted in Middle Eastern studies to conclude that the flow of influence might have moved from China to the West.

The third level of Europeans with an interest in China consisted of those who were essentially popularizers, and they came to dominate the eighteenth-century view of China. They were interested neither in a cultural accommodation between Chinese and European cultures as part of a missionary strategy, as were the Jesuits, nor in a serious intellectual approach that would yield advances in knowledge, whether it be the *Clavis Sinica* of Müller and Mentzel or the creation of universal forms of knowledge pursued by Leibniz. Rather, Europeans on this third level were interested in finding in China support for European political and intellectual movements, particularly the Enlightenment. This was the most superficial of the three levels of interest in China and it produced the greatest distortions of Chinese culture. In short, European knowledge of China over the years 1500–1800 did not continue to evolve but rather after 1700 degenerated into the superficialities of exploitation by a European cultural movement followed by a negative reaction against this superficial image of China.

Travel literature was in great vogue during the seventeenth and eighteenth centuries. Part of the interest was based on a curiosity about unusual and remarkable lands and people, much like the interest in science fiction in our own age. But there was a practical side to this interest as well, because the information gained from travel literature was also useful to commerce. The new societies of learning in Europe, such as the Royal Society of London, combined intellectual and commercial interests. And yet European knowledge of China was so limited that it was possible for an imposter like George Psalmanazar (1679–1763) to succeed in meeting with the Royal Society in 1703 and (for a time) to be accepted as a native of Taiwan (Formosa). His book, *An Historical and Geographical Description of Formosa,* appeared in London bookshops in 1704 and immediately became a best-seller in England, France, Germany, and Holland, although it was a complete fabrication written by someone who had never been to East Asia.

Psalmanazar's book was written in a style favored at that time for travel literature, namely, a colorful first-person account with many illustrations. It successfully combined a description of an exotic land and people with a polemical attack on the Jesuits, which in the overheated atmosphere of the Rites Controversy played well with the Jesuits' many enemies. The illustrations included a map of Formosa that bears only the most general likeness to reality. Psalmanazar described in detail an invented language that he called "Formosan" and presented illustrations of Formosans who look remarkably European (see figure 5.1). He included drawings that depicted a Formosan funeral and emphasized the idolatry and human sacrifices of the Formosan religion, whose god (depicted in the form of an ox or elephant) demanded the hearts of eighteen thousand young boys every year. Fittingly, it was the Jesuits who eventually unmasked Psalmanazar as an imposter.

Louis Cousin (1627–1707) of France had been destined for service in the church, but after studying theology and law, he obtained a sinecure as the presiding officer at the Court of the Mint in 1659. This position gave him a secure

The Funeral, or Way of Burying the Dead Bodies

Fig. 5.1. Drawing of a supposed funeral in Formosa from *An Historical and Geographical Description of Formosa* (London, 1704) by the imposter George Psalmanazar. Permission of the Institutum Historicum Societatis Iesu, Rome.

income in return for few duties and enabled him to concentrate on his intellectual interests. In 1687 he became editor of one of the earliest periodicals, the *Journal des Savants*, to which he contributed until 1701. Academic honors came in 1697 with his election to the French Academy. As editor of the *Journal des Savants*, Cousin handled many reports and book reviews dealing with China. Consequently, when *Confucius Sinarum Philosophus* was published in 1687, Cousin appears to have seen a chance to broaden readership by translating the work from scholarly Latin into more readable French and condensing it to more popular dimensions. (One must emphasize that he is only the apparent author; this condensed work, like many works of that time in Europe, was published anonymously and Cousin's authorship is probable rather than definite.)

The resulting work, *The Morality of Confucius (La morale de Confucius)*, was published in Amsterdam in 1688, only one year after the appearance of *Confucius Sinarum Philosophus*. The fact that the Jesuits had labored on their translation for a century reflects some of the differences between how these two levels of Europeans with an interest in China (the missionaries and the popularizers) approached their field. Although Cousin distorted the historical Confucius by exaggerating his rational qualities, he was merely reproducing the overly rationalized image of Confucianism presented in *Confucius Sinarum Philosophus*.

The same could not be said of another popularized work about Confucius. The Frenchman Nicolas-Gabriel Clerc (1726–1798) continued a family tradition in medicine by becoming a physician to eminent noblemen and their military units. In 1778 he was called to Versailles to become the national inspector general of hospitals. Whereas Cousin occupied a largely literary world, Clerc moved in the highest political and social circles of the ancien régime in France and Russia. When the French Revolution began, Clerc turned to literary studies and especially to writing a six-volume history of Russia. His concern with moral nurturing on the very highest political and social level was reflected in his sole publication on China in 1769. *Yu the Great and Confucius: A Chinese History (Yu le Grand et Confucius, histoire chinoise)* was dedicated to the grand duke of Russia (later Czar Paul I, who was assassinated in 1801). Given the dedication, it is perhaps not surprising that in the very year of the book's publication Clerc received a dual appointment in Russia as physician to Grand Duke Paul and director of the corps of cadets. In his dedication to *Yu the Great and Confucius,* Clerc exhorted the fifteen-year-old czarevitch to emulate Yu the Great as the "prototype of morals of his nation." Clerc presented Yu as the father of his subjects who through his own behavior made the Chinese virtuous. Clerc reinforced his royal exhortation by noting that both Russia and China ruled vast territories.

What is striking about this book is the frank manner in which Clerc admits to fictionalizing Chinese history. Yao, Shun, and Yu were a famous trio of rulers in Chinese antiquity who were said to have established the principle of selecting rulers on the basis of morality and ability rather than birth. Clerc was aware that Yao, Shun, and Yu were three consecutive kings, yet he attributed actions of all three to Yu. (Many scholars today believe that these three kings are legendary rather than historical, but they were presented by most European sources of Clerc's time as historical.) Next, by juxtaposing two figures from Chinese history who were not contemporaries, Clerc created an anachronism. He knew that approximately seventeen hundred years separated the lives of Yu the Great (r. 2205–2198 B.C.) and Confucius (551–479 B.C.), although he believed that the reader would excuse his fiction because of its necessity to the plan of his work. Another way in which Clerc fictionalized history was by choosing a legendary figure like Yu the Great, about whom very little was known, and then fabricating details about his life. The fact that much more was known about Confucius was not significant to Clerc, who was less interested in presenting the historical details of these two figures than in using them as models for the didactic instruction of the young Russian prince.

His delineation of Yu the Great and Confucius as models ("the best prince and the greatest philosopher of the Empire of China") reveals how much Clerc shared the values of the Enlightenment. Clerc presented them as models who exemplified one of the central tenets of that movement: in order to improve men, it is necessary only to enlighten them. Implicit in this statement is the assumption that knowledge by itself would lead to moral improvement. However, this is not exactly what Confucius taught. Clerc presented Confucius as a teacher of virtue, but he misinterpreted Confucian love as being egalitarian and universal in the Christian manner when in fact it is carefully defined by gradations of age, rank, and familial relationship. Clerc described the process by which Yu came to the throne as something very much like the philosophes' enlightened monarch consulting with an intellectual. Specifically, the legendary emperor Shun was said to have invited Confucius to share his crown, and when Confucius modestly declined that honor, he recommended to Shun the name of Yu, whom Confucius regarded as the most worthy man in Shun's realm. When Yu attempted to decline on grounds of inability, Shun granted him a four-year grace period in which to be instructed by Confucius. This, of course, never happened except in Clerc's fictionalized account.

The Enlightenment's Idealization of China's Morality and Political System

Whereas the initial impetus for promoting Chinese culture in Europe had come from the missionaries, by the eighteenth century the driving force behind this promotional effort became the anti-Christian philosophes of France. Although called by the French term for "philosophers," the philosophes were really journalists who used the new popular written media of pamphlets and books to promote their cultural agenda. Although opposed to Christian proselytizers, the philosophes proselytized with equal fervor for a different point of view. In the philosophy of Confucianism, certain philosophes found elements that corresponded closely to the ideals of the Enlightenment, and these Confucian elements were promoted enthusiastically in Europe. However, the promotion of Chinese culture in Europe gave rise to some opposition, and not all philosophes were Sinophiles (enthusiastic admirers of China and its culture). Consequently, there was a tension throughout the Enlightenment between Sinophilia and Sinophobia (dislike of Chinese culture).

One great irony was that in their treatment of China, the philosophes were forced to rely upon a group whom they sought to displace as molders of intellectual opinion in Europe. The philosophes had an extremely optimistic view of the power of human reason and they believed that religion, such as Christianity, that relied on divine revelation and faith was the cause of many of the problems in society. In the eyes of the philosophes, the chaos and killing of the Reformation and Counter-Reformation could have been largely avoided if more emphasis had been given to human reason than to irrational religion. The philosophes sought to replace Christianity (a religion of revelation) with deism (a religion of reason). Deism teaches the immortality of the soul and the belief that God created the world but does not actively intervene in the world's running, except for an occasional fine-tuning, as in adjusting the time on a clock. In fact, the mechanical clock is a good metaphor for deism. One winds it up and it runs on its own. Since God does not actively intervene in the world, there is no reason to pray to God for intervention.

As representatives of revealed religion, the Jesuits embodied the antithesis of the deistic (or sometimes atheistic) framework that the philosophes sought to establish as the dominant intellectual mode in European society. Yet the Jesuits continued to be in the eighteenth century, as they had been in the seventeenth century, the most knowledgeable sources of information on China. The Jesuits who had traveled to China and lived there for years had acquired a deep and direct knowledge of Chinese culture and its leading philosophy, Confucianism. Practically none of the philosophes had visited China. They were like those Jesuits, Charles Le Gobien and Jean-Baptiste du Halde, who remained in Europe, editing the material received from the China missionaries and casting it into the most favorable light for promoting Jesuit propaganda. Although du Halde was a Christian and Voltaire was a deist, both could be characterized as committed believers and talented China propagandists.

The first Enlightenment thinker to extol the Chinese was the German Christian Wolff (1679–1754). In 1721 Wolff expressed this admiration in a controversial lecture at the University of Halle, a center of Christian Pietism, which was the antithesis of Enlightenment deism. Inspired by Leibniz, who had died in 1716, Wolff borrowed the idea of the "practical philosophy" of the Chinese, which Leibniz had explained in terms of ethics and politics. Wolff believed that the Chinese practical philosophy (i.e., Confucianism) contained a rational ethic that was both logically consistent and offered practical benefits to the individual and society. Wolff and the later French philosophes shared the view that Confucianism was capable of establishing an ideal form of government; furthermore, Confucianism confirmed their belief that it was possible to have morality without Christianity. Like many of the philosophes, Wolff denied that he was an atheist and claimed to be a deist.

Because of this lecture, China became the focus of a controversy between the Enlightenment rationalists and the Christian Pietists. Wolff's Pietist colleagues criticized his presentation of Chinese philosophy on the grounds that it fostered atheism. They also criticized Wolff, a professor of mathematics, for not limiting himself to his primary field of expertise, although the polyhistor tradition—so admirably embodied in Leibniz—must have offered some justification for Wolff's delving into the realm of Chinese philosophy. The ensuing intellectual and political struggle has been oversimplified as one between religious fanatics (the Pietists) and their rationalist victim (Wolff), though recent scholarship has pointed out that the Pietists were not irrational and actually believed that learning and religion could be harmonized. Wolff's victimization was probably accentuated by the fact that he lost the political struggle when King Frederick William I expelled him from Prussia. Although Wolff had relied primarily upon Jesuit works on Confucianism, he projected his own anti-Christian beliefs onto his interpretation of Chinese philosophy. Like the French philosophes who followed him, Wolff disregarded the subtleties of Chinese philosophy and religion and subsumed China's culture to the Enlightenment's cultural agenda.

Through the influence of Voltaire (the pen name of François-Marie Arouet, 1694–1778) and other philosophes, China's morality and politics began to displace China's language and history as an important influence in Europe. Voltaire's primary sources of information on China were the numerous Jesuit works on China whose tone was favorable and whose contents emphasized Confucius and his philosophy. In his article on China in his *Philosophical Dictionary*, Voltaire bestowed exaggerated praise on China as a land of the greatest antiquity, surpassing any in Europe. He rarely passed up a chance to criticize the Jesuits. Confucius was said to have voiced the purest morality. Voltaire defended the Chinese against the charges of atheism and idolatry. He claimed that their religion was free from superstition and absurd legends, clearly implying that Christianity is filled with such things. Voltaire revealed his subtext when he claimed that the Chinese worshiped one God and were in communion with the sages of the world whereas Europe was divided into many groups of hostile Christians. In short, this idealized view of China is what Voltaire wished a religiously divided post-Reformation Europe to become.

Voltaire and other Enlightenment thinkers argued that China was a model enlightened monarchy in which the emperor ruled by the rational values of Confucianism. This required that the monarch consult with the scholar-official class, a characteristic essential to the ideal of an enlightened monarch that was promoted by the Enlightenment. Voltaire believed that the cultural spirit (*esprit*) of the Chinese Confucian scholar-official elite could be an ethical and political model for Europe.

Also enthusiastic about China were the Physiocrats, whose leader was François Quesnay (1694–1774), a physician to Louis XV. In the aftermath of France's disastrous defeat by England in the Seven Years' War (1756–1763), the French sought ways of regaining their lost status. Quesnay, who became known as the "Confucius of Europe" because of his great admiration for the Chinese philosopher, expressed his proposals in a small work entitled *The Despotism of China (Le despotisme de la Chine)* (1767). In this work Quesnay advocated emulating the Chinese model in reorganizing the French economy around agriculture. Quesnay admired the way that Chinese scholar-officials were given power in the manner of Plato's *Republic* in which philosophers became kings. His admiration of a minimum of government intervention in the Chinese economy was the basis on which the Physiocrats originated the phrase *laissez faire* (let things alone) in an economic context. In reality, the Chinese emperors tended to intervene extensively in the work of officials.

Differing Views of Polyhistors and Philosophes in the Encounter with China

Although Leibniz and Voltaire admired many of the same things about China, the nature of their admiration was different. Leibniz's thinking was shaped by the seventeenth-century polyhistor model, which cultivated knowledge in a broad range of fields rather than a primary expertise in one field. Whereas our own age would regard the knowledge of polyhistors as superficial, the polyhistor model would regard today's experts as too narrowly focused to comprehend the connections between the various parts of knowledge and unable to grasp the connections needed to attain a comprehensive view of the whole. With a scholar of average ability, the polyhistor model does degenerate at times into superficiality. However, in the case of a brilliant mind, such as Leibniz, this ability to understand the broader connections in knowledge is truly remarkable.

When Leibniz applied his polyhistor mentality to studying China, he achieved some remarkable insights. In fact, one could argue that the European understanding of China was deeper in the century preceding Leibniz's death in 1716 than in the following century. Leibniz was closer to the proto-Sinological approach, which tended to be serious and scholarly. However, the philosophes were more interested in promoting a particular intellectual program in which reason would replace religion than in developing a comprehensive understanding of China. Many philosophes saw China as proof that reason in morality and politics worked; they praised the Chinese for selecting their officials on the basis of scholarship and they extolled the Chinese system of government for fostering the development of enlightened monarchs, such as the Kangxi Emperor, who they believed ruled in consultation with the scholar-officials. The philosophes admired the Confucian morality, which taught right and wrong without revealed religion. In fact, the philosophes practically adopted Confucius as their own sage.

Using another culture to advance a cultural program is not the most objective way to understand that culture and inevitably results in its distortion. While the philosophes' interest in China was cosmopolitan in that it drew some of its models from outside the Judeo-Graeco-Christian tradition, it sought, not to understand China for its own sake, but rather to exploit China for the promotion of the philosophes' program. While it is unrealistic to think that any approach to studying another culture is purely objective, there are degrees of objectivity. In spite of the rather astounding misunderstandings of scholars like Müller and

Mentzel and despite Müller's interest in financial remuneration for his Clavis Sinica, their focus on the Chinese language gave them a degree of objectivity that was greater than that of the philosophes. Although Leibniz did not himself undertake a serious study of the Chinese language, he was very much interested in a Clavis Sinica that might enable him to learn quickly to read Chinese. Among the eighteenth-century contemporaries of the philosophes in France, scholars such as Nicolas Fréret (1688–1749) and Joseph de Guignes (1721–1800) took a serious interest in the study of China and its language. Although they might be characterized as proto-Sinologists, they nevertheless subsumed their study of China to European concerns rather than studying China in its own right.

The philosophes' less objective interest in China made their interpretations of China more vulnerable to European cultural forces that had nothing to do with China. These cultural forces led to a division among the philosophes in their attitude toward China. Those philosophes who saw elements of Confucianism as corresponding closely to the Enlightenment's cultural program were enthusiastic in promoting the model of China in Europe. These Enlightenment thinkers included Wolff, Voltaire, and Quesnay. They could be characterized as Sinophiles. Other leading philosophes, such as the baron de Montesquieu (1689–1755) and Denis Diderot (1713–1784), were critical of China. Montesquieu viewed the government of China as a despotic system maintained by the threat of violence in the form of the cane. In his famous work *The Spirit of the Laws* (1748), Montesquieu defined three basic types of government: republican, monarchical, and despotic. While the republican government was motivated by virtue, the monarchy was based on honor, and despotism was grounded in fear. Montesquieu took issue with the predominantly favorable Jesuit accounts of the Chinese government because he felt that the Jesuits had been misled by the appearance of political and social order in China. Montesquieu argued that the spirit of the Chinese government was dominated by fear. Montesquieu and Diderot could be characterized as Sinophobes. Throughout the Enlightenment there was a tension between Sinophilia and Sinophobia. At the beginning of the eighteenth century, Sinophilia predominated, but by the end of the century the pendulum of fashionable enthusiasm had swung decisively in the other direction, toward Sinophobia.

The division of Enlightenment thinkers into Sinophiles and Sinophobes reflects the philosophes' shallow understanding of China. Sinophilia and Sinophobia belong to the categories of enthusiasms while proto-Sinology and Sinology belong to more neutral and objective categories of thought. Because the Enlightenment's understanding of China was built on shallow foundations, it was more vulnerable to the shifting tides of intellectual fashion. Sinophilia could (and did) easily give way to Sinophobia, a common phenomenon in the history of cultural encounters between China and the West. Although the Jesuit missionaries' approach was also shaped by their own program, namely, their effort to convert the Chinese to Christianity, they had seriously studied the Chinese language and its culture and would consequently remain throughout the seventeenth and eighteenth centuries the most knowledgeable and leading authorities on China. Not until the temporary dissolution of the Society of Jesus in the years 1773–1814 and the development of Sinology with the establishment of academic chairs at European universities in the early nineteenth century (beginning in Paris in 1814) would the Jesuits be displaced from this position.

How the Chinese Changed from White to Yellow

Ethnocentrism (the belief in the superiority of one's culture) has been present in history since antiquity and was very much a part of Chinese history. However, theories of racial superiority are a relatively new phenomenon in world history. The division of human beings into races based on color (black, red, white, and yellow) first emerged in the eighteenth century.

Although the notion of four human races was not developed until fairly recently, discrimination on the basis of skin color had been known since antiquity. Perhaps the earliest instance of skin-color discrimination is found in India. The ancient Hindu work *Rig-Veda* (ca. 3000 B.C.) describes an invasion by light-skinned Aryans from the north down into the Indus River Valley and their conquest of the indigenous dark-skinned people. These skin-color differences were eventually incorporated into the Hindu caste system under which lighter-skinned people were awarded a higher caste than darker-skinned people. In the West, there is an Old Testament tradition of racial differences supported not by Scripture itself but by Hebrew oral tradition preserved in the Talmud. This tradition was often cited to explain the blackening of the skin of Africans as punishment for the sins of their ancestor Canaan, whose father was Ham and whose grandfather was Noah.

Europeans' changing attitudes toward China over the years were reflected in their perception of Chinese skin color. These changes have been traced by the German historian Walter Demel. Europeans who admired the Chinese referred to their skin color as white, while those who held the Chinese in low esteem regarded them as less white, or yellow. In sixteenth- and seventeenth-century European writings, references to the Chinese as white predominated, but as the eighteenth century progressed, they were increasingly described as nonwhite or yellow. The division by Europeans of the world's inhabitants into four or five races was the fruit not only of an increasing knowledge of the world's surface gained through exploratory voyages but also of Europeans' military and economic ascendancy over other peoples, an ascendancy that became more pronounced over the course of the seventeenth and eighteenth centuries.

Nevertheless, the idea of dividing human beings into races was not readily accepted by European thinkers until the eighteenth century. In 1655 the French Calvinist Isaac de la Peyrère (1596–1676) published *Pre-Adamites (Praeadamitae),* in which he claimed that there were two separate creations in Genesis. The first chapter of Genesis speaks of the creation of a man and woman who are not named while the second chapter refers to the creation of Adam and Eve. Peyrère interpreted this to mean that two separate races were created: humans who preceded Adam, and humans who were descended from Adam. He claimed that the pre-Adamites were Gentiles and the Adamites were Jews, that is, God's chosen people. Peyrère's book was condemned by the censors and he was imprisoned for his heretical beliefs. He was released only after issuing a public retraction of the theory. He traveled to Rome to ask for the pope's blessing and renounced his Protestantism. However, there is some evidence that he continued to hold these views in private. Peyrère's theory was very influential on eighteenth-century deists, who used it to justify their belief that the nonwhite peoples of the world (Africans, Americans, and Asians) were pre-Adamites and inferior to the descendants of Adam. The latter in the seventeenth and eighteenth centuries included Christian Caucasians as New Testament descendants of the Old Testament Hebrews.

The Italian Alessandro Valignano, S.J. (1539–1606), played a crucial role in formulating the Jesuits' mission philosophy of accommodation in East Asia, which challenged the Eurocentric understanding of Christianity. In a report of 1577 Valignano showed that he shared the Iberian lack of respect for the cultures of Africa, India, and Southeast Asia and was pessimistic about Christianity's chances of becoming inculturated in these areas. However, he was much more optimistic about the prospects for Christianity in Japan and China, whose cultures he viewed as equivalent to Europe's. Valignano referred to the Japanese and Chinese as "white people" *(gente bianca).*

The Iberian *Reconquista* had fostered in Spain and Portugal a concern with purity of blood that took the form of anti-Semitism, but this was not exactly the same as racism, in which skin color determines dominance. Such racial theories were developed in the eighteenth century by a considerable number of the most eminent thinkers of Europe and the United States, including Thomas Jefferson. The division of mankind into four or five races began with the Frenchman François Bernier, who published his *New Division of the Earth (Nouvelle division de la Terre)* in 1684. In the eighteenth century, Peyrère's theory of the pre-Adamites was revived and exerted tremendous influence on Enlightenment thinkers. In 1740 the Swede Carolus Linnaeus claimed that there were four races, which he associated with skin color: Europeans were white, Americans red,

Asians yellow, and Africans black. Shortly thereafter, in 1749, the Frenchman George Buffon drew parallels between skin color and level of civilization.

The Scottish philosopher David Hume published a work in 1777 that claimed that of the four or five species of humans, only those with white skin were civilized and the nonwhite species were inferior to whites. The first to elaborate a theory of a "yellow race" was the German philosopher Immanuel Kant, who did so in works of 1775 and 1785. Kant believed that this yellow race consisted mainly of Hindu Indians who intermarried with Mongols to produce the Chinese. The philosophe Montesquieu, whose low opinion of Chinese culture was mentioned earlier, referred to the Chinese as yellow. These were only the initial theories of racial differences. The full implications of racial superiority and inferiority would develop only gradually, reaching their peak in the West during the high point of European imperialism in the late nineteenth century. At that point, the Chinese were seen in hostile racial terms by many in the West as the "Yellow Peril." This term expressed a fear that the great numbers of the yellow race threatened the existence of the white race and Western civilization.

The Macartney Mission to China (1792–1794)

The year 1800 marks the end of a cycle in Sino-Western relations. Very soon after 1800 a series of humiliating military defeats and diplomatic submission would show China's glory to be a thing of the past. But even before 1800 there were signs that China's glory was ebbing. One of the clearest of these signs came through the observations of the Macartney mission to China in the years 1792–1794.

At that time the British East India Company held a state-granted monopoly among English companies on trade with China. However, because of the restrictions imposed by the Chinese government in the Cohong system based in Canton, trade with China during the years 1770–1780 had not been increased. In an attempt to improve its trading position, the East India Company had sent an embassy to China in 1787–1788, but the death of the head of the mission en route caused the embassy to abort. Nevertheless, in England the potential trade with China was viewed as so great that another embassy was planned. In 1792 George Lord Macartney was appointed "Ambassador Extraordinary and Plenipotentiary from the King of Great Britain to the Emperor of China."

Unlike so many of the overbearing and incompetent English noblemen involved in diplomacy and the military during that time, Lord Macartney (1737–1806) was ideal in many ways. Of average height and pleasant manners, he had been regarded as one of the most accomplished and handsome young men of his day. In his active life as a public servant, he demonstrated a stable temperament, reliability, firmness in dealing with opponents, honesty, and integrity. He had scholarly tastes and was not without courage. When the French attacked Grenada in 1779, Macartney as governor was carried as a prisoner back to France. In a duel fought in 1786, he was seriously wounded. He served with distinction at the court of Catherine the Great in Russia, in the West Indies, in Ireland, and in India, where he developed a good working relationship with the directors of the British East India Company. He was also favored by the British prime minister, William Pitt. Consequently, he was an ideal choice to head an important embassy to China.

Macartney was assisted by an equally capable diplomat, Sir George L. Staunton (1737–1801). Macartney and Staunton were born in Ireland in the same year. Staunton completed his medical studies in France and attained note as a writer on medical subjects. He was a friend of the famous Dr. Johnson. He purchased an estate in Grenada, where in 1779 he met the newly appointed governor, Macartney. This was the beginning of a long and close friendship. When the French attacked Grenada, Staunton also was imprisoned and carried with Macartney back to France, where he negotiated Macartney's release. The bond between the two men was formed, and in 1781 when Macartney went to India to serve as the governor of Madras, Staunton accompanied him as secretary. After he returned to England, Staunton became very close to Edmund Burke. His scholarly achievements were recognized with his election to the Royal Society in 1787. When Macartney was appointed minister plenipotentiary to head the embassy to China, Staunton was appointed not only his secretary but also provisional plenipotentiary with the authority to replace Macartney should the latter become incapacitated or die. It was intended that Staunton should eventually serve as British ambassador to China, but illness prevented him from carrying out that assignment.

The Macartney mission was meticulously planned. Since no interpreters trained in Chinese were available in England, Staunton had to travel to the Chinese College founded by Father Ripa in Naples to find two Chinese students who would serve as interpreters for the embassy. He secured the services of Paolo Cho and Jacobus Li (alias Jacob Plumb), both of whom had finished their study for the priesthood and were ready to return to China. They were able to translate in Chinese, Italian, and Latin but not English. Father Cho left the embassy when it landed at Macau in June 1793 and traveled overland to rejoin it in Beijing in September. Father Li was more steadfast and remained with the embassy throughout. Li is said to have had a brother who was a scholar-official. Upon the embassy's return from Beijing, Li remained in Macau, though he later sent letters written in Latin in 1801 and 1802 to Macartney. Li was praised by Macartney for his capable and honest service.

When Staunton traveled to Naples to secure the interpreters, he was accompanied by his eleven-year-old son, George Thomas (1781–1859). The young

Staunton later accompanied the embassy and studied Chinese with Fathers Cho and Li. Eventually, he would exchange a few words of Chinese in the audience with the Qianlong Emperor. In addition to the two interpreters, the eighty-four-member mission included six musicians, a machinist, infantrymen, a botanist, and the artist William Alexander, whose prints and watercolors have provided a visual record of the embassy. A collection of high-technology presents for the Chinese emperor was carefully selected. These included chemical, electrical, and mathematical instruments as well as pieces of Wedgwood pottery. The aims of the embassy were to facilitate trade by reducing or abolishing export-import duties, open ports other than Canton to trade, stimulate a Chinese interest in more British products, secure a small piece of land for use as a British trading depot and residence, and gather as much information as possible about China.

The lead ship, a sixty-four-gun man-of-war called the *Lion*, departed Spithead, England, in September 1792 and sailed to the west across the Atlantic and then down the coast of South America and finally across the Pacific to the shores of Canton, where it arrived in June of 1793. Using the diplomatic pretext of wishing to present birthday presents to the Qianlong Emperor on his eighty-third birthday, the embassy won an invitation from the Beijing court to sail northward and land at Dagu. The Chinese expended a considerable amount of money toward the transport and daily allowances of the Macartney embassy. In one sense, the Chinese saw Lord Macartney as representing a tribute envoy of higher than ordinary status. In another sense, he was viewed in traditional Chinese diplomatic terms that regarded foreign ambassadors as representing submissive nations that came bearing tribute and requesting benefits from the emperor in return. Consequently, the banner on Macartney's barge clearly identified him in Chinese as a tribute-bearing envoy from England.

Although Great Britain rejected this traditional Chinese framework of diplomatic relations, Macartney's diplomatic skills made him realize that it would be unwise to make an issue over the banner. Later, however, after being conducted from Beijing to the emperor's summer residence in the cooler climate of Rehe, Macartney did make a point of refusing to perform the *koutou*, an elaborate bow in which tribute-bearing envoys kneeled and touched their head to the ground in obeisance to the emperor (see figure 5.2). Instead, Macartney merely went down on one knee. Nevertheless, the Qianlong Emperor observed the niceties of formal politeness. He received the letter from King George III of England, exchanged gifts with his visitors, sent his guests some food from his table, and said farewell. Realizing that his imperial audience was over, Macartney desperately tried to open negotiations with Heshen (1750–1799), the power behind the throne, but to no avail. After several days of tours, the embassy was escorted

Fig. 5.2. The Approach of the Qianlong Emperor to the reception of the English ambassador Lord Macartney, Rehe (Jehol) in Manchuria, 14 September 1793. Printed with the permission of the British Museum (London), Department of Prints and Drawings.

back to Beijing and, after receiving several broad hints that it was time to leave, they reluctantly departed from the capital on 9 October.

In retrospect, the meeting of the Qianlong Emperor on that glorious, brisk morning of 14 September 1793 in Rehe foreshadowed an autumn that transcended the weather. Although the glory of China was still evident—in the majestic setting, the elaborate tent, the hordes of attendants, and the ability to control the foreign embassies—the signs of decline were present. Even the appearance of the emperor himself was deceptive. The emperor, who was about to celebrate his eighty-third birthday, was described by Macartney as looking twenty years younger. In fact, the Qianlong Emperor was growing senile. His senility had produced an infatuation with a young imperial guardsman whose handsome features reminded him of a lost concubine. This was Heshen, corrupt and corrosive, who helped hasten the China of the late eighteenth century into its decline.

Some of these signs were apparent to Macartney, who compared China to an enormous drifting ship, in danger of going aground. Although the Macartney embassy was a diplomatic failure, it did obtain information that, for the British East India Company, justified the expense. This information was put to good use in Great Britain's ascendancy over China during the next two centuries until its ouster from Hong Kong in 1997.

Conclusion

By 1800 the great encounter between China and the West was over. It ended because of the remarkable ascendancy of the West over the rest of the world through exploratory voyages, technology, and colonialism and because China itself had entered into a steep decline. Because of their success, Europeans and their descendants in North America thought of themselves as too far advanced to find much of substantive value in a backward nation like China. Unlike pre-1800 adulatory references to "the great and mighty kingdom of China," Westerners now spoke of the "inscrutable Orient." China became an object of merely exotic interest because of its past and was no longer important as a source of current knowledge. A few Westerners continued to admire Chinese culture and to study it seriously, such as the famous missionary-Sinologist James Legge (1815–1897) of the London Missionary Society, who made a monumental translation of all nine Chinese classics. However, the numbers of these Westerners were so small and their impact so slight that they could be dismissed as students of merely curious subjects.

Whereas Chinese culture had been admired and emulated during the previous two centuries, it now became an object of ridicule and scorn. The Chinese became identified with a rigid adherence to backward tradition. Confucianism was seen as a fossilized vestige of the past. The Chinese people were looked upon as belonging to a yellow race that was inferior to whites. Even the Chinese characters were looked upon as exotic antiques that were obstacles to modern learning. (In the 1950s the Chinese government came to the brink of abandoning the characters for a phonetic script.) That period of disdain for China is now at an end and a new period is beginning. Predicting the future is a most uncertain task, and yet it seems clear that future encounters between China and the West will have far more in common with the ebb and flow of reciprocal influences of the period 1500–1800 than with the Western arrogance and Chinese humiliation of 1800–1997.

Works Cosnsulted

Appleton, William W. *A Cycle of Cathay: The Chinese Vogue in England during the Seventeenth and Eighteenth Centuries.* New York: Columbia University Press, 1951.

Bodde, Derk. *China's Cultural Tradition: What and Whither?* New York: Holt, Rinehart & Winston, 1957.

Demel, Walter. "Wie die Chinesen gelb wurden: Ein beitrag zur Frühgeschichte der Rassentheorien." *Historische Zeitschrift* 255 (1992): 625–66.

Dictionary of National Biography: From the Earliest Times to 1900. Edited by Sir Leslie Stephen and Sir Sidney Lee. Vols. 12 & 18. London: Oxford University Press, 1937–1938.

Foley, Frederick J. *The Great Formosan Impostor.* Taipei: Mei Ya, 1968.

Gossett, Thomas F. *Race: The History of an Idea in America.* Rev. ed. New York: Oxford University Press, 1997.

Macartney, George. *An Embassy to China, being the Journal kept by Lord Macartney during his Embassy to the Emperor Ch'ien-lung 1793–1794.* Edited by J. L. Cranmer-Byng. London: Longmans, 1962.

Mackerras, Colin. *Western Images of China.* Hong Kong: Oxford University Press, 1991.

Maverick, L. A. "Chinese Influences upon the Physiocrats." *Economic History* 3 (1938): 54–67.

McKee, David Rice. "Isaac de la Peyrère, a Precursor of Eighteenth-Century Critical Deists." *PMLA* 49 (1944): 456–85.

Mungello, D. E. "Aus den Anfängen der Chinakunde in Europa, 1687–1770." In *China illustrata: Das europäische Chinaverständnis im Spiegel des sechszehnten bis achtzehnten Jahrhundert,* edited by Hartmut Walravens, 67–78. Weinheim: Acta Humaniora, 1987.

———. "Confucianism in the Enlightenment: Antagonism and Collaboration between the Jesuits and the Philosophes." In *China and Europe: Images and Influences in Sixteenth to Eighteenth Centuries,* edited by Thomas H. C. Lee, 99–127. Hong Kong: Chinese University Press, 1991.

New Catholic Encyclopedia. New York: McGraw-Hill, 1967–1979.

Popkin, Richard H. "The Philosophical Basis of Eighteenth-Century Racism." In *Studies in Eighteenth-Century Culture.* Vol. 3, *Racism in the Eighteenth Century,* edited by Harold E. Pagliaro, 245–62. Cleveland: Case Western Reserve University Press, 1973. See also in the same volume "Symposium Introduction," 239–43.

Reichwein. Adolf. *China and Europe: Intellectual and Artistic Contacts in Eighteenth-Century Europe.* Translated by J. C. Powell. London: Kegan Paul, 1925.

Ross, Andrew C. *A Vision Betrayed: The Jesuits in Japan and China, 1542–1742.* Edinburgh: Edinburgh University Press, 1994.

Wolff, Christian. *Oratio de Sinarum philosophia practica: Rede über die praktische Philosophie der Chinesen.* Translated by Michael Albrecht. Latin and German texts. Hamburg: Felix Meiner, 1985.

Index

About the Author

D. E. Mungello, the grandson of Italian and German immigrants to the United States, completed his doctorate at the University of California at Berkeley. His research in Sino-Western history led to three years of study in Germany as an Alexander von Humboldt fellow and Herzog August Bibliothek fellow. He has published several books, including *Curious Land* and *The Forgotten Christians of Hangzhou*. He is the founder and editor of the *Sino-Western Cultural Relations Journal*. His first teaching position was at Lingnan College in Hong Kong, and he currently is professor of history and director of Asian studies at Baylor University in Waco, Texas.